Sunflowers
on Market Street

*Stories of Offenders and How They
Transformed a Neighborhood*

by

E. Gail Chandler

This book is dedicated to

My Parents, Jess And Ruth Wilson

And is in memory of
Father William Diersen
Founder Of Dismas Charities Inc.

Contents

Acknowledgments

Dismas Charities Inc. provided support for the writing of this book. Without the encouragement of Chief Executive Officer Ray Weis, Executive Vice President Jan Kempf and the Board of Directors, this publication would not have become a reality. While Dismas Charities sponsored the project, opinions expressed are my own and not necessarily those of the organization.

A retirement gift from Administrative Assistant Jane Sherer, a collection of all the human interest stories I had written at St. Patrick, provided the inspiration to proceed with a manuscript. Mrs. Sherer and Joe Lane, assistant director of Dismas Charities St. Ann, retyped my stories and stored the files on computer disks, an invaluable aid in the writing process.

A special thanks to all the individuals who edited and gave writing advice through the years, most particularly Al Russell, Kathlene Bello, Bob Yates, Steve Smith, John Lentz, Stephen Wrinn, Steve Vice, John Brown and my husband and daughter, Curtis and Tara Chandler. Thanks to Gene Henchey for keeping my computer running and to my editor, Mary Pat Nimon.

The St. Patrick assistant directors Jennifer King, Kathlene Bello and Yvette McCollum and the staff maintained a steady course for the center, which enabled me to devote time to the special projects covered in this book.

My father, Jess Wilson, a twice-published author, has followed closely the development of this book. While not accepting his proposed title, *The Repentant Thief,* other advice from him and my mother, Ruth Wilson, was invaluable. My appreciation for their parenting, generosity and wisdom has grown through years of watching individuals ravaged by neglect and abuse.

Dr. Judi Densen-Gerber, executive director of Odyssey House in New York, provided an education on the anti-social personality disorder, which has been invaluable throughout my career. Her belief that these individuals can change has provided hope during dark times.

Thanks to Barbara Jones, deputy secretary for the Kentucky Justice Cabinet, for writing the forward, to Kathlene Bello and Rocco Dilbeck for contributing their stories and to former wardens Betty Kassullke and John Bill Dotson (deceased) for mentoring.

Finally, this book would not have been possible without conversations with incarcerated men and women over many years. For each individual, there is a story. Some experiences were not included because of the author's quality of writing, others because of confidentiality and still others because the proper words to describe their situation never came. I want to thank the men from St. Patrick and to assure those who cannot find their story that they also are important.

Forward

Gail Chandler had been at her new job with the Kentucky Correctional Institution for Women (KCIW) for one week when she was served with a federal civil rights class-action lawsuit. She was named one of the defendants solely because she had recently been named the deputy warden.

The plaintiffs, a group of female offenders, claimed that the conditions under which they were confined were unconstitutional. As general counsel for the Kentucky Department of Corrections, I called Gail and notified her that she must appear with the prison warden at the federal courthouse in Louisville, Kentucky. I was to be her attorney, but we had never met.

Anyone else would have wondered if she had made a bad career move. But Gail Chandler faced the challenges head-on. This litigation became the primary focus of her professional life for years to come. It was the catalyst for positive changes for the female offenders, the KCIW staff and the corrections system in Kentucky. KCIW became a national model facility for female offenders, and Gail became a corrections expert in management, program development, classification, security, construction and litigation.

Who is Gail Chandler, the author of this book? She was my client and she became my very dear friend. You do not go through years of intense litigation, produce a roomful of documents, sit through days of depositions, provide facility tours for experts plus a federal judge and sit through weeks of trial without getting to know each other very well. At the time, Gail essentially had two full-time jobs — deputy warden and defendant. Fortunately, because of the kind of person Gail is, we became friends, not enemies. Certainly, the latter was possible.

Gail possesses a unique quality that comes from her experience as a manager, educator and counselor: She has an uncanny ability to know her clients better than the clients know themselves. She possesses a genuine belief that there is good in everyone and that people can change if that is what they want. However, she is not easily fooled – she recognizes resistance and deals with it accordingly. Gail has succeeded in the corrections field where others have not because she enjoys the challenge it provides her, and she loves the people and her work. In short, she is committed to the people who need her, the offenders.

How fortunate were those offenders who were supervised and counseled by Gail, for she worked in their best interests. How lucky were those of us who worked with Gail, for she taught us to never give up. I can say with certainty that Gail is admired by most and respected by all. Enjoy her book; it truly comes from her heart.

Barbara W. Jones, Deputy Secretary for
the Kentucky Justice Cabinet

Prologue

The gray stone school building sat precariously on the side of a mountain in Eastern Kentucky. In the seventh-grade classroom, a boy in tattered clothing sat in the back. With a mop of unruly brown hair and a severe case of acne, he looked older than his classmates but struggled with his work. Each time the teacher left the room, he took the opportunity to pelt his fellow students with paper wads. The year was 1954, and while adolescents in the same class — including myself — achieved varying levels of success, the boy in the back of the room became a statistic in the world of corrections.

At the close of the 20th century, there were 1.3 million people in state or federal prisons in the United States and an additional 5 million in jails or under community-based supervision, probation or parole. Ours is one of the highest incarceration rates in the world. The federal government predicts that one in eleven men will be imprisoned during his lifetime and one in four black men. Obviously, they are not all Ted Bundy's or John Wayne Gacy's. Who are the people behind the statistics? Frequently, they resemble the troubled boy in the back of the classroom, a symbol of individuals known by most of us.

After a career of almost thirty years working with the incarcerated, I do not have an answer. The incarcerated come in all colors, from all cultures and from all economic levels. For some, incarceration results from a life completely out of control. It is comparable to being on a speeding train and knowing that the bridge is cut. Arrest is viewed with relief. Incarceration can be a substitute for suicide.

Self-control cannot be taught by complete loss of freedom, which is comparable to building muscle by complete bed rest. While complete loss of freedom may be needed in some cases to protect the public, it should not be confused with treatment. It has been my experience that community corrections, accompanied by counseling, can be very useful in teaching postponed gratification and reducing the chances of additional offenses.

After working in a New York City facility for drug offenders and later as a child welfare supervisor, in 1976 I became Kentucky's first female deputy warden of a male prison — an eighty-bed facility in

Frankfort. There, I developed a career-long habit of spending time each day on the yard, talking with inmates, gaining confidence and experience, as well as learning the language and humor. After two years, I moved to a larger minimum-security prison and later to the Kentucky Correctional Institution for Women (KCIW).

At KCIW, I unknowingly walked straight into a class-action lawsuit on conditions and discrimination against women in prison, *Canterino v. Wilson*. This lawsuit became one of the two most significant federal cases on the rights of women prisoners in American history.

During the thirteen-year course of the litigation, it was necessary to examine every operational aspect of Kentucky's male prisons, including the state maximum-security prison at Eddyville. At Eddyville, my work even included conducting an independent study of death row, assuring the conditions were comparable for our one female death row inmate.

During my tenure, the KCIW population grew from 123 to more than 500, KCIW became accredited under the standards of the American Correctional Association, and five major construction projects were designed and completed. Federal court released KCIW from monitoring in record time.

In 1993, I became the first female deputy warden at Kentucky State Reformatory (KSR). KSR is a 1,400-bed, medium-security male prison and was one of the two oldest prisons in Kentucky. In my mind, the facility held a certain mystique; it was a "real" prison. Surrounding the 130-foot guard tower, forty acres were secured by double fencing covered with rolls of razor ribbon. Gun towers were located around the perimeter. The prison also quartered the majority of Kentucky's mentally ill prisoners, referred to in past decades as the "criminally insane."

A few days prior to my retirement from KSR, Dismas Charities Inc. offered me the opportunity to become director of St. Patrick, a community correctional center. Dismas Charities provides care for offenders through contracts with state or federal agencies. It was founded in 1964 by Father William Diersen, a Roman Catholic priest involved in prison ministry at Kentucky State Reformatory, who was distressed by the lack of resources available to inmates with no family or community support. With help from the Louisville councils of the Knights of Columbus, he opened a fifteen-bed community correctional facility. He called it Dismas, named for the repentant thief who was crucified with Christ. Today, Dismas Charities is one of the nation's largest private, not-for-profit providers of social services.

The mission of Dismas is to "heal the human spirit," a philosophy compatible with mine. I had great respect for this agency and accepted the position. Six years working with community-custody inmates at St. Patrick rounded out a career of daily contact with offenders at every custody level.

At the time I was director, Dismas operated five facilities in inner-city neighborhoods in Louisville, Kentucky. Dismas Charities St. Patrick, which housed male residents, was located in a Civil War-era Catholic church on Market Street, a downtown industrial area. When the congregation moved to a suburban location, Dismas renovated the building and reopened it in 1993 as a community correctional center. Its design for residential use had both blessings and limitations. The sunny yellow walls, high ceilings and stained-glass windows provided a stark contrast to prison decor. The limitations became evident more gradually as new residents felt the breezes from the massive windows and realized that conversations echoed throughout the building.

Residents ranged in age from eighteen to their early seventies. While the state prison population ratio by race is approximately sixty-two percent white and thirty-eight percent black, the ratio at St. Patrick was usually the reverse for two reasons: The percentage of prisoners in the lower custody ratings is higher for black inmates (in part because of the number incarcerated for drug sales). The second reason is that efforts are made to place offenders near their home of record, and a high percentage of black Kentuckians live in the metropolitan areas of Louisville and Lexington.

St. Patrick staff consisted of about seventeen people, a director, assistant director, administrative assistant, two or three counselors and eleven part-time or full-time resident monitors. Resident monitors provided direct supervision similar to correctional officers in a prison.

All Dismas Charities directors were required to complete certain essential tasks each month. These tasks included fire drills, searches, file audits and the submission of a human interest story for use in communicating with the Board of Directors and for public relations. Writing the human interest story quickly became my favorite. Through writing, I could vividly illustrate the varied events that swirled around us each month. It was a way to bring to life the challenges faced by our staff and residents. At the end of six years, I had more than seventy vignettes describing people, situations, obstacles — and a picture of how these Dismas residents changed the face of their neighborhood through community service work.

The events in this book are taken from those stories and are as true as I could capture them. However, the vignettes were written in an environment where new facts could be discovered after writing was complete and other facts were never uncovered. Many names and identifying details have been changed to protect the innocent (and the guilty). Although in practice residents usually are addressed by "Mr." and their surname, they are referred to by first names throughout this book, both in the spirit of anonymity and to differentiate them from staff.

This book describes some of America's 6.3 million offenders, their daily life in a community correctional setting and the contributions these individuals can make. It is my hope this book also raises larger questions about our nation's current criminal justice policies.

Legal status of St. Patrick residents

Nearly forty percent of Kentucky offenders are classified as eligible for supervision in a facility without fences. The majority of people incarcerated will be released, and certainly, the percentage moves to almost 100 percent among those with minimum- and community-custody ratings. For these offenders, alternatives to incarceration are the most effective and add no substantial risk to the public. These are the inmates who are least explored in popular prison literature.

Experts say that placing an offender in the least restrictive environment his custody rating allows is the best correctional practice for several reasons. The cost is normally lower at facilities at the lower security levels. It is more productive for the non-violent and unsophisticated. And appropriate programming is simplified when inmates are of a similar custody level.

Residents came to St. Patrick in one of three legal statuses: pre-release (inmate), parolee or halfway back.

The **pre-release residents** are community-custody **inmates.** They came to St. Patrick through transfer from another correctional facility. To be eligible, an inmate had to be within eighteen months of a parole board hearing or serving out the end of his sentence. If, upon meeting the parole board, an inmate was given a new parole board meeting date instead of release, he could stay at St. Patrick if the deferment was not longer than eighteen months. It was possible for a pre-release resident to remain several years in the facility.

Inmates at Kentucky correctional facilities are not permitted to accept gainful employment. The Department of Corrections allows inmates to participate in community service when certain correctional policies and procedures are met. Approved community service programs vary from highway cleanup to clerical work and can only be provided to a state, federal, city or approved non-profit agency. For a day's labor, the inmate receives $1.25. This stipend is called "state pay" and is very important to the indigent.

Parolees have been granted parole. Some requested placement at St. Patrick in lieu of a home placement. Some of these parolees had no family support. Others were required by the parole board to complete a community center program before release to a home placement. The parolee program lasted about two months and included securing gainful employment, opening a savings account and finding a home placement. The parolee moved to home placement after successfully completing the program and after his parole officer approved his living arrangements. Parolees comprised about forty percent of St. Patrick's population.

A **halfway back** is a person under parole or probation supervision who has been placed in a community correctional center as an alternative to incarceration. While the issues bringing offenders into the halfway-back program vary from failure to maintain employment to loss of a home placement, the underlying problem is usually substance abuse. The parole officer sends the offender to the program with instructions to spend thirty, sixty or ninety days and to accomplish assigned goals such as acquiring employment and completing a substance-abuse program. This ten percent of St. Patrick's population was the most problematic and required a disproportionate amount of staff time and energy.

– PART ONE –

The Faces

    Mostly it is the residents I see in my memories, black, white, old, young, gifted, challenged, handicapped, strong and whole, laughing, crying, conning, truthful, selfish, generous, hardworking, lazy, neat, messy, abused, abusive, hopeless and rewarding. On good days, their faces reminded me of sunflowers.

Dismas Charities St. Patrick

Ghosts

In 1971, I returned to Kentucky from New York City, beaten by the "Big Apple." I had accepted a job in Prestonsburg. Located in far Eastern Kentucky, Prestonsburg is firmly situated in the Appalachian Mountains. Unpacking, I wondered if I had lost my mind in Manhattan, but I had no desire to repeat those experiences, ranging from assault to cockroaches and unemployment. It had taken twenty-one years to get out of Appalachia, and here I was back. Over the next three years, I developed a new appreciation for the land and the people. This peace did not extend to the discoveries found in my new employment.

For five years (three in Prestonsburg and two in Bullitt County, located near Louisville), I worked as a child welfare supervisor. We made decisions daily that affected the lives of children. We did this without knowing all the parts of the various puzzles that included abuse, neglect, poverty, alcoholism, retardation, spouse abuse and hopelessness. Mistakes were easy, and the consequences were frequently serious. I had trouble sleeping. I saw the children in my dreams. At the end of five years, I resigned without another job or a plan. I knew only that I could not do that job any longer.

Four months later, I joined the Kentucky Department of Corrections. Corrections was a good fit. I grew accustomed to clanging gates, large keys, handcuffs and gray-green paint. Over time, I developed techniques for communicating with prisoners. I was comforted by the fact that while adult offenders do not always act maturely, they are adults and legally responsible for their own behavior. No longer carrying the responsibility and the guilt for the outcome of lives, I did my best and slept well. I worked at four Kentucky correctional facilities before retiring from state employment and coming to Dismas Charities as the director of St. Patrick in 1995.

Not only was the atmosphere different from corrections, but the agency had a mission similar to mine: to heal the human spirit. In the relaxed atmosphere, I found time to talk at length with residents and counseling staff. In these last years of my career, I deepened my understanding that all of us — staff, community members and offenders — are products of our experiences.

Experience with children who were abused helped me understand adult behavior. By reviewing files and reading about residents' family history, I looked for clues about the person behind the criminal behavior. Sometimes the scars of child abuse were found in unexpected places.

Edwin arrived at St. Patrick three weeks before Halloween. Blond, age forty and intense, he looked like an accountant, not a parolee. While he quickly located employment and followed the rules, something seemed amiss. He wore the prison clothing he arrived in until he received his first paycheck, a sign of little family support. He had no

St. Patrick, Louisville

visitors. He did not make friends. He continually complained of minor inconveniences and did so in detail. He did not laugh or smile. The only person he talked to was his counselor, and his counselor one day talked to me about her concerns.

She told me that Edwin's brother, ten years his senior, raped Edwin at age four. A year or so later, the brother added various forms of torture. When Edwin was eight, his brother made him eat lye, causing permanent digestive tract malfunctions. The brother sexually abused him through most of his teenage years.

Edwin's counselor arranged specialized treatment for abuse survivors. His relationship with his counselor remained important. He still did not smile or laugh. His relationships with others did not improve until an encounter with Luke on the night of the Halloween party.

Luke was a farmer, all farmer. Among his crops, he found marijuana to be especially profitable. His decision to diversify led to his incarceration. Even at St. Patrick, where he resided for several years as an inmate, he found a way to farm. In a deserted plot next to a railroad underpass, he planted squash and tomatoes. By a barbwire fence in an industrial area, he planted sunflowers. Beyond his need to grow plants, his appearance and personality radiated the stereotype of a man of the soil. He was short, sturdy and taciturn. He refused family support because he figured he had made the mistakes, not his family. This left him without funds.

Luke

The prize for the best Halloween costume at the annual Halloween party was $20. It was a fortune to Luke. His best friend Jack, and Jack's girlfriend Ann, had a mutual, but warped, sense of humor. Ann proposed that Luke dress up for the party as Pippi Longstocking, a guaranteed winner. Ann could not find a Longstocking costume but came up with something almost as outrageous, a pumpkin suit.

Halloween night found Luke on the backyard in a bright orange pumpkin suit stuffed with numerous pillows. He could not move properly and had to lean back in a chair in the manner of a woman nine months pregnant with a ten-pound child. Green vines grew around a sour-faced Luke.

Edwin arrived on the backyard, escaping from the children cavorting around the center. Edwin saw Luke. First, he gasped. Then, he pointed to Luke. He giggled and snorted. The giggles grew into full-blown laughter. He cried with laughter. He exploded with laughter. He kept laughing. Forty years of laughter came out. The laughter was contagious, and soon every resident and visitor on the backyard was laughing. Edwin would walk back inside, only to return later, and again he would point at Luke and laugh.

Luke won third prize. Expecting him to be disappointed, I returned to the backyard later in the evening to see how he was holding up. He was smoking a cigarette and thoughtful.

"It was worth it," he told me. "That man has not smiled since he got here, it was every bit worth it."

Luke picked up his stomach and walked back into the center.

While Edwin's problems were far from over, he began making friends. His demeanor relaxed. He made progress in counseling. He graduated from the program at St. Patrick and was released. The last I heard, he was doing well.

Edwin represents countless children currently living in abusive situations. He represents thousands of adult child-abuse victims currently in our country's prisons. He represents the importance of treatment in our efforts to resolve the complicated issues of crime and justice. He represents the adults in our nation living with the ghosts of child abuse.

An Unmixed Blessing

Jack arrived early one January with two other pre-releases, Denny and Casper. The arrival of pre-releases (or inmates) was normally of more significance than the arrival of parolees or halfway backs. Men of the last two types seldom were at St. Patrick for more than three months. Inmates could initially be at the center for up to eighteen months and if deferred by the parole board, more than two years.

When the three walked through the door, I happened to have two Christmas packages left, each containing a number of useful items. They managed to allocate the gifts based on who had the greater need for each item. This made me hopeful; still, I could not predict the future. On that day, they were just three unknown entities.

Casper, age twenty-six, stood five foot two. Prematurely balding, his hair did not match his round, childlike face or diminutive body. Prone to temper tantrums and impulsive behavior, he would end his stay by escape.

Denny, age forty, was a former salesman. Alcohol and a cocaine habit cost him his job, his wife and his home. Denny found religion in prison and felt it his duty to convert everyone he met to his exact beliefs — the only possible correct ones. A hustler, he made beds, washed clothing and performed any task he could think of to make money from his less energetic peers. Being told that this was against the rules in no way affected his behavior. The world was wrong and he was right. He composed and sang with his guitar. His positive opinion regarding his talent was definitely a minority one. But he did have some positive attributes. Denny was not afraid of heights. During his stay, he cleaned the cobwebs from every corner of the high cathedral ceilings. He worked hard and energetically at every assignment. Still, I spent a good percentage of my time listening to others complain about him and still more trying to convince him that I was, in fact, the director.

Jack appeared just a bit too tall, even-featured and sociable to be a computer nerd. But he had computer experience and a variety of maintenance skills. At thirty-two, he was the father of six children from several relationships. (His mother told me that Jack should be smart enough to figure out what was causing all of those children.)

Jack and Casper spent their second day at St. Patrick painting a bathroom. One of them put the dirty paintbrushes behind the dumpster. When I found the brushes, they were ruined. The color of the paint meant that either Jack or Casper was responsible for the destruction. Both of them denied guilt and blamed the other. In a few weeks, I learned enough about their characters to be assured Jack was not the guilty party.

Jack

From the day Jack painted the bathroom until release, he was never without a project, an idea, a joke, a unique observation and unbounded enthusiasm. In a world of depressed, selfish and angry people, Jack was sunshine.

Jack was placed immediately in a community service position working for the most exacting supervisor in any of the agencies providing work placements for St. Patrick inmates. Jack became his right-hand man. The department administrator later selected Jack to be an administrative assistant, still making the state pay stipend of $1.25 per day. He received almost daily compliments from his supervisor. The manager of the city agency promised Jack a full-time position when his incarceration ended.

Jack always was available to help in the center as well. He informed me when furniture, fixtures and appliances were broken. If he could not make the repairs, he usually knew another resident who could. He created sign-up sheets for recreational activities, adjusted the thermostats and let me know when supplies were low. He volunteered his time and energy wherever needed. When there was a major break in the water main, Jack, Luke and another resident worked late into the night, in mud, to assure that the facility had water. He worked endlessly on neighborhood landscaping projects, and through his contacts with the city agency where he worked, he secured the necessary tools.

St. Patrick's front sidewalk

Over the next year, Jack helped with some major projects. His father became an unofficial volunteer. Together, he and Jack designed the cover for the resident rulebook, loaned us an old hearse for the Halloween party, donated items for resident Christmas boxes, designed a golf scramble booklet and printed the covers. Jack took over the decorating for Halloween and Christmas using old materials and new ideas. The haunted house that year was incredible. By his assumption of responsibility, my job was infinitely easier.

Perhaps the most positive contribution Jack made was to the Alcoholics Anonymous program. Because volunteer outside speakers were sometimes unreliable, I requested that residents hold their own AA meetings. Previous residents swore this would not work, but Jack, with his leadership abilities, pulled it off. Outside speaker or not, we now always had meetings, coffee and a program. Jack started a tradition that remained. Upon Jack's release, the AA leadership passed to Omar, a square-shouldered black man with fourteen years of sobriety. Between Jack and Omar, a number of men made serious commitments to sobriety.

Part of the adventure of working at St. Patrick was the ever-unfolding cast of characters. Casper, Denny and Jack arrived the same day with no introduction. Daily contact gradually revealed their characters and personalities. Casper brought grief and disappointment. Denny brought a complex array of feelings, from frustration to amusement. Jack was an unmixed blessing. When he was released, the transition was eased with the arrival of Omar and others. (Their experiences after they were released were similarly varied and can be found in the Epilogue.)

Can I Take My Daddy Home?

Omar was a forty-year-old black man, flawlessly groomed with a glint of gold in his teeth. He was a former railroad worker with fourteen years of sobriety. He made other residents melt with the strength of his personality. As an inmate who had not yet made an initial parole board appearance, his stay at St. Patrick would be about two years. The first time Omar came to my attention was when several residents gave me a review of an Alcoholics Anonymous meeting. Apparently, Omar had attacked the lack of standard traditions in the meeting and the informal atmosphere. On the night in question, there had been no speaker. The usual AA leaders were defensive but conceded that, not only did this new resident have a point, but he had many contacts in the outside AA community and potentially could be of assistance.

The next week, I had a brief conversation with Omar. I explained that Jack, the AA chairman, had made a breakthrough by arranging regular meetings chaired by residents. He indicated his interest in helping. He reviewed his years of sobriety and the contacts he had in the AA community in Louisville. I was impressed by his sincerity, maturity and commitment to the program.

When Jack paroled, Omar became the new AA chairman. He added many traditions to the weekly meetings. He would walk through the center just before an AA meeting and in a deep baritone loudly announce, "Attention all alcoholics, attention all alcoholics!" While residents are not allowed to have control over each other, staff supervision of the meetings was intermittent. Residents were habitually late. The sign-in sheet started going in Omar's pocket after a short grace period at the start of the meetings. The sheet would re-emerge at the end of the meeting. The other residents did not complain. Not only did they understand how seriously Omar felt about AA, but his personality was intimidating.

Attendance at AA meetings improved. Residents arrived and departed in a more timely manner. The speakers were impressive. Some men who previously appeared to have no redeeming social value were reading the "Big Book" of AA and taking part in the meetings. To assure the center gave proper priority to AA, Omar joined the recreation committee responsible for planning monthly events.

While Omar's objective on the recreation committee was the scheduling of AA events, he also started taking part in other center activities. He found this important because his wife and son, Li'l Omar, visited regularly and came to center activities.

AA meeting area

Children's play area for visitation

Li'l Omar, age six, was a miniature reproduction of his father. Bright, personable and verbal, he became a favorite of staff and residents. Well behaved, he did not create the kind of havoc for which some young visitors were famous. While firmly under the control of his parents, he was treated with respect. He was a well-loved child, reportedly achieving well in school and popular with his peers. (Li'l Omar gave me the report on popularity.)

A few months after Omar arrived, the center held a St. Patrick's Day party. Li'l Omar participated in the children's games, won some prizes and demonstrated his athletic skills. He also broke a counselor's heart.

The counseling staff normally helped with parties. Tana Crosby was in her office, located a short distance from the visitors' restroom. Ms. Crosby, in her early thirties, was a child of the sixties who spent her early years in a commune. With long blond hair and a quick smile, she was easily approachable and her door was open.

Li'l Omar came to Ms Crosby's door. "I want to talk to you," he said. While somewhat taken back, she invited him to come in. He went behind her desk and started, "I want to take my daddy home." After he received a stammering response, he continued, "I won't keep him long, just a little while…."

Ms. Crosby attempted to explain why this was not possible.

"I'll bring him right back." Ms. Crosby knelt, and he looked her straight in the eyes. "Please…," he said, as he closed his eyes and tears came through his lashes.

His were not the only tears as she walked him from the room.

After Ms. Crosby reported this event to me in detail, I thought about it for months. I determined that, when sufficiently prepared, I would have a serious talk with Omar. Deciding that an appointment would add importance to the conversation, I scheduled an evening.

Omar was unprepared for the intensity of my tirade. "You have a serious problem with your ethical system," I started. "You have job skills, you have an adequate education, and you know the principles of AA. When you are released, are you going to live them? You have been sober for fourteen years. You do not have the excuses of the addicted. You committed the crime that brought you to prison after you became sober. Selling drugs to others was strictly and absolutely greed. You caused damage to others, the addicted and their families. Certainly they might have purchased from others — they didn't, they purchased from you!" The paint seemed to be peeling from the walls, and I remembered the tears in Li'l Omar's eyelashes.

After I calmed down, we talked. Omar discussed an obsession with lifestyle. We discussed the value of people versus the value of things. We talked a long time. Before he left, I extracted a promise that he would review his ethical system in the quietness of his bed.

The next day, Omar told me he had slept little. Through the grapevine, I learned that ethics was a topic in the next AA meeting. Omar entered substance-abuse treatment with a professional.

Six months after I retired, I learned that Omar was still the AA chairman at St. Patrick. In a few months, Li'l Omar would get to take his daddy home. Omar had the knowledge he needed to be a responsible citizen. In a fictional story, they would live happily ever after. In the real world, the ending is yet to be written.

Harry's Hemorrhoids

Harry, a thirty-seven-year-old parolee, had a fierce exterior. At six foot four and 230 pounds, he was a weightlifter whose muscular arms were highlighted by an ever-present white T-shirt. A face pitted with old acne scars completed his overall rough appearance, and he resembled a bouncer or a bit player in a prison movie. It is easy to overlook needs in such a man.

Offenders frequently have difficulty with problem-solving. A resident who is hell-bent on solving a problem his way because he desires a certain pre-selected end is much different than a resident who truly cannot solve a problem. Walking a resident through this second type of problem can be a strange journey. Such was the case of Harry's hemorrhoids.

Parolees are responsible for their own medical care. Some of them have little experience managing this care and paying for it. As staff members, we try to assist in finding appropriate, reasonably priced options without, of course, practicing medicine.

One evening, I was leaving St. Patrick late, both tired and generally annoyed at the world. It was almost 9 p.m. Residents seemed to have radar that went off as we prepared to leave the building. It was then that they had to talk to us about something very important. Harry caught me going out the door.

"Mrs. Chandler," he said. "I must talk to you about something really important."

I stopped just outside the front door and he followed. "I am bleeding from the rectum, bad!"

I asked him if he thought he needed to go to the emergency room.

"No."

"It appears you need to go see a doctor tomorrow."

"I have to work."

"You will need to take off."

He suddenly burst into loud and anguished sobs, bending over in an attempt to control himself. I then resolved that I would not be going home anytime soon.

"Let's talk," I said, directing him to the bench in front of the center. After he calmed down, I started asking questions.

"Do you have a history of hemorrhoids?"

Conversation benches

He indicated that he did. He went on to tell me how he had a total work-up "with a scope and everything" while at Bell County Forestry Camp, a state minimum-security facility. He said that the hemorrhoids were not bad enough for surgery, and they found nothing else wrong in his intestines.

"What color was your stool today?"

"Yellow," he replied.

"What did you do at work today?"

"I moved a hundred refrigerators."

"Did you ever use Preparation H?"

He said medical personnel at Bell County gave him some and it helped a lot. I asked why he had not purchased any. He said he didn't know what to buy.

I told him about immediate care centers and that this type of service was much less expensive than emergency rooms. We then went inside to see if we could locate, by telephone, an open immediate care center. We could not. I told him to go in the bathroom and check to see if he was still bleeding. He came out and gave me the news, "just a little bit."

I asked him if he wanted to go to a drug store and get medication. He did. The only drug store that was open would close before he could get there by bus. We checked, and the Walgreens at Eighteenth and Hill was still open. "Come on," I said. "Sign out."

As Harry signed out, I told Shelia at the desk, "If my husband calls, tell him I went out with a man."

We all laughed. I knew that in the same situation, my husband would do the same thing. (We spent the early months of our marriage picking up drunks, his clients, and hauling them to detox. More than one threw up in our car.) Off we went to Eighteenth and Hill to get Preparation H.

When we got there, I picked out a generic brand ointment. I sent him on to the cashier's desk so he would not be embarrassed. We headed back to the center.

The next day, Harry told me he was much better. He never did go to the doctor, so apparently the medication worked. Healing takes many forms. Sometimes it is the human spirit. And sometimes, it's just hemorrhoids.

Beetlejuice and "The Kid"

I heard about Beetlejuice before I met him. I called the center to check in, and Administrative Assistant Jane Sherer answered. Mrs. Sherer, a grandmother of Scandinavian descent with a marked Wisconsin accent, always could be counted on to provide an update on the latest events.

She reported, "We got a parolee in who is a little weird. He just finished doing twenty years. He is a real artist. The residents call him Beetlejuice."

I found this interesting. Not only are artists frequently helpful in assisting with center activities, but a man who had served twenty consecutive years would require added support.

A few days later, I called the new parolee in for an interview. I understood his nickname at once. Beetlejuice fit perfectly. In his early forties, he was a slim, anxious white man. His left ear, pierced seven times, held a collection of various hoops. He wore a tightly bound head rag and carried his billfold on a chain. His clothing seemed three sizes larger than his body. He might have once been nice looking, but his strange trappings overshadowed his presentation. There was something wounded about him that was hard to define. I did not learn much about him except that he reported he served his time for burglary. It seemed strange to me that he had served such a long sentence for this charge. I thought there must be more to the story and made a mental note to review his history as I conducted the required monthly file audits.

I settled in the next week to audit files. Of all the tasks I did as a director, this was my least favorite. I had such a hard time staying on task that I sometimes jokingly asked the staff to lock me in my office. It was a break when I reached the file I wanted to see. When I reviewed Beetlejuice's arrest record, I saw it. He received a new charge while in prison, adding time to his sentence. Eighteen years ago, while serving time at a 1,400-bed, medium-security prison, Kentucky State Reformatory (KSR), he and another inmate assaulted a man named Samuel Elliot Rogers. "Samuel Elliot Rogers," I said aloud to an empty office. Twice.

Samuel Elliot Rogers was not only a jailhouse lawyer of notoriety, but he was the most infamous sexual predator in the Kentucky correctional system. He was in my unit many years ago in his brief and singular stay in minimum-security. I remembered watching with distaste as he stalked young first offenders. I also recalled reading a letter from a woman regarding his parole request. She wrote, in part, "He is like a father to my three teenage sons." I stopped work and shared the information on Beetlejuice with his counselor.

A few days later, I saw Beetlejuice in his counselor's office. We discussed KSR, where I had worked and Beetlejuice had served his sentence. I said, "I saw you had an encounter with Samuel Elliot Rogers." I then muttered, "Perhaps they should have given you meritorious good time."

"I was twenty-four when Rogers came after me," he said.

A few days later, I got a look at Beetlejuice's artwork. It was good but macabre. He was excited about Halloween and painted a grim reaper on a party prop, the vampire's casket. A circle of residents watched him work. Among them was another amateur artist called "The Kid."

"The Kid" had just turned nineteen and was serving his time at St. Patrick, an environment much different than Beetlejuice had experienced at the same age. Usually the youngest man in the center, he had

died. He did not know what to do, so he committed a burglary and waited to return to prison.

Michael's academic education was limited, and he could barely read or write. He was dumb…"like a fox." He was skilled at serving time. He spent a good deal of time in the center's smoking area, a frame shelter covered with plastic and known as the "smoke tent." For months, he prospered in the marathon smoke tent poker games. He was an equal-opportunity poker player, taking money from whoever joined the game.

There are several vices not far from any correctional environment. Drugs and alcohol brought eighty to ninety percent of our clients to us. In order to operate a facility where residents can heal, drugs and alcohol must be defeated. This required constant vigilance. Fortunately, we had some very good tools to help us. Drug screens, a drug detection dog, a handheld alcohol sensor and an alert staff can keep these problems to a minimum. Gambling is a different story.

While investigating an allegation against a staff member, I had an enlightening conversation with a resident about gambling. I individually interviewed six men alleged to have participated in a poker game. As I was more determined to discover the truth about the staff member than punishing the six participants, I granted them immunity and only asked that they tell the truth. Each told me the same story. The last man added some interesting commentary. He told me that he wasn't worried because he knew I would find out. He said, "These men gossip like seventh-grade girls. I knew you would put a stop to it." He went on to say that gambling is a "man thing." I knew there was some truth to this.

In every organization where men are gathered, gambling seems to be present in one form or another. Gambling can be very detrimental in a correctional facility. Men can run up debts. Violence can occur. Families suffer when they are using hard-earned money to pay gambling debts of residents. Through the grapevine, I always made sure I knew the status of gambling at St. Patrick. After the incident, the staff member resigned. Gambling ceased for a time.

Then Michael St. John came to St. Patrick. For a while, his games had very small stakes. While vaguely aware of the recurrence of this unauthorized recreational activity, staff attention was elsewhere. We had a temporary drug problem to be resolved. (Michael's name also was mentioned in this activity). At the resolution of the drug problem, six men left — some absconding, some discharged — but all were involved with drugs. Those absconding knew that they would be taken into custody when their drug screens came back. Michael was lucky.

We had a serious staff meeting about the responsibility of our positions. After the meeting, I told one of our staff members, a retired Army first sergeant, that the poker club had gone on too long and suggested he stake out the smoke tent from a hidden location, listen to the game and write up those involved. He called me at home and in military fashion attached a name to his plan: "Operation Tent Shield." He and another staff member went into the smoking tent hourly, shook down everyone there, counted their money and generally made their lives uncomfortable.

The poker games ceased. One man thanked the staff, saying he could now keep his money. The smoking tent returned to a place of smoke and gossip. Michael admitted the error of his ways and had a temporary run of good behavior.

Realistically, what were the chances that Michael could change his life? His risk profile score gave him about a fifty percent chance of making it. Given the lack of positive role models in his life, low self-esteem, rule violations and being successful at only one thing, doing time, I think the estimation was overly optimistic.

Yet…rarely a week passed when I did not have several visitors, men who completed the program and were successful. Some of these men had odds like Michael St. John. Offenders do not come with warranties. Still, occasionally miracles occur, and perhaps this is a reason that some believe in a patron saint of lost causes.

The smoke tent

A Pearl of Great Price

When I graduated from high school forty years ago, I received a string of cultured pearls from my uncle and aunt. I did not believe the pearls were expensive, as my relatives were not wealthy people. Not identifying with this type of jewelry, I relegated the pearls to a dresser drawer for most of the next thirty-eight years. My uncle developed financial problems, and they lost their business and their farm. They left the Appalachian area of Kentucky. My uncle died in Cincinnati. He was forty-six years old.

One day I took out the pearls, remembered my uncle and decided to have them re-strung. On a lark, I also had them appraised, thinking all the while that the price of the appraisal would be more than the pearls. When I picked up the necklace and received the appraisal, I was shocked. I recalled the biblical parable of *A Pearl of Great Price*.

I wear the pearls often now. I touch them and think about my uncle and aunt, their struggles and their incredible humor and sweetness. I also think of a St. Patrick resident, for a reason I will explain.

Each person is a miracle. The series of events that led to our individual births defy all odds. It is especially so in this country, where we have resulted from the blending of many cultures and ethnic origins. When I look at my daughter, I have renewed understanding of these odds. An ancestor on her father's side was a Frenchman who grew to adulthood in England and then immigrated to this country. Her father's grandmother was a full Cherokee. This lineage also includes Italian and English. On my side, ancestors include Dutch fishermen, Mennonites, Scotch-Irish, Native Americans and African-Americans.

My husband and I met her at birth with joy and welcoming. I look at her and see a miracle, a Pearl of Great Price.

Job also was a Pearl of Great Price, but the circumstances that met his birth were far different. A biracial child, he was the only one of seven siblings with an African-American father. He never knew his father's name. His mother rejected him at birth, a rejection as total as a baby bird thrown from the nest because it looked different. His maternal grandmother, an alcoholic, took him in. She was not capable of caring for him, and his childhood was chaos. The court declared him neglected, and he moved in and out of foster care, placements with relatives and his grandmother's home. He graduated to prison. At twenty, he was a confused young man with large brown eyes, a warm smile and skin the color of toffee.

Biracial residents arrive at St. Patrick with some regularity. It is understood that there are many very successful biracial people, the most obvious example being Tiger Woods. It is just as surely a fact that those who end up in our care have additional baggage, a lack of clarity about their identity. Rejection based upon their very existence is not unusual. It took until 2000 for the U.S. census to acknowledge biracial Americans. In American society, one is black or white, not both.

Job's grandmother died while he was at St. Patrick. With all of her inadequacies, she was the only mother he had ever known. His counselor took him for a final visit at 3 a.m. He wept bitter tears and spent the night discussing the pain of his youth and the place she had in it. He knew he soon would be alone in the world.

Dismas Charities is in the business of healing the human spirit. We will be here until every child is loved, nourished and wanted. We will be in this business until every child is recognized as a Pearl of Great Price. We will be here a long time.

How Long Is Twenty-Eight Years?

Bob had been incarcerated for twenty-eight years when he arrived at St. Patrick. He was in the initial stages of processing when I arrived at work one morning. We recognized each other from Kentucky State Reformatory. We had a brief conversation, and he told me how long he had been in prison. Later in the day, I thought about Bob and decided to interview him and capture his story in writing. I wanted to concentrate on the time he served, what happened to him, the importance of a transition plan for him — and the implications of a long prison sentence, in light of our society's desire to incarcerate people for longer terms. A personal interview was mandatory for understanding the man behind the extended prison sentence.

A week after he arrived, I called Bob to my office and asked to interview him, explaining the purpose of our talk. With carefully parted, thin, gray hair, a pale gray-white complexion and intense deep-set gray eyes, he was devoid of color — but not personality. Tall and lanky, he still wore the tan prison-issued clothing usually shed like a snakeskin on the day of arrival, except for cases of indigence. The uniform was starched and pressed. He agreed to the interview, and we spent an hour and a half in deep conversation.

He began his sentence in 1968 at age thirty-two. He ended his sentence in 1996 at almost sixty. He served time in seven Kentucky prisons, the first thirteen years at the maximum-security prison in Eddyville. He spent about nine years at Kentucky State Reformatory in three different stays. He had a heart attack. He had a deep spiritual awakening. He became a correctional observer. Prison became his life. It was all he had.

Describing the impact of twenty-eight years, he said, "It's more than a lifetime, it's a living death. My younger life is gone. I lost my family, my work, my friends and any hope of acquiring material things. I rolled myself up. I trusted no one. I knew loneliness. I learned to do without. The world inside prison became my only world. I knew I had to forget about the streets. People must live with reality. They cannot live inside dreams. I tried not to escape into a dream world, a black pit. I knew this was a risk. I had to establish a life."

We talked about how people survive long sentences and the importance of an income, a life's work, the canteen and a room that becomes a home. I talked about discussing these issues with young offenders facing long sentences and about how they could best make a life.

He talked about his own spiritual awakening. He said that there was nothing to his left or right and only ghosts behind him. He didn't believe in rehabilitation, because that implies that there is something to bring back. He experienced a complete spiritual change, in heart, mind and attitude. He said that the most help came from a young minister at Eddyville, the state maximum-security prison, who brought him along in the only way possible, through tiny steps.

Bob explained that over the years, in spite of his spiritual awakening, bitterness and hatred grew. He said he had the choice of letting it out a little at a time or allowing it to eat him up inside. He did not want someone innocent hurt because of his anger. He also became extremely compliant with authority, always staying away from people and trouble, always avoiding conflict. He felt that coming to St. Patrick had been very therapeutic for him.

He described his first day out as an explosion. The explosion was the total impact of the changes, the cars, the streets, the people, the tall buildings and the fact that there was not a stationary tower. The first thing he noticed about St. Patrick was the security door, and he felt as if he had been transported back to prison. He said he asked permission to come into the office area by the Central Monitoring Office (CMO) and others looked at him strangely, because it was an open area. He said when he saw me, a familiar face from KSR, he knew he would be all right.

Bob's second day was even more stressful. He referred to it as his "little monster day." He had to go to the parole office by himself. As he walked down the street, he saw a police car. He turned and started to run. Then he saw the car was gone. He forced himself to turn back around and continue his walk. When he arrived at the parole office, he saw more parked police cars. He told himself, "It's not you that they are after. It's all a ghost. It is bad memories come to life. It's not real."

The biggest leap in realizing freedom came when Bob found a job. As his last prison state paycheck had arrived and been cashed at the center, during his first lunch hour, he went to a gas station to buy a cake and a coke. Suddenly, it occurred to him that he had money in his hand and it was strange. A co-worker came out with a quart of beer. Bob felt shock go through him as he realized that there was beer in the store. It was so forbidden. He had to force himself to go back in the store the next day. He said, "If a horse throws you, you must get back on. I had to prove to myself that I could go in the store and get what I wanted."

Bob discussed the importance of having a warm, supportive, friendly, environment to help him get on his feet and reduce the anger built up in prison. St. Patrick filled this need. Not only had the staff been nurturing, but some of the other men answered his questions and provided friendship. It occurred to me that Bob was exactly who Father Diersen had in mind when he requested help to found a halfway house called Dismas.

Society is demanding that courts incarcerate individuals for longer and longer terms. It appears there should be recognition of, not only the fiscal cost to lengthy sentences, but the human cost as well. If we incarcerate people throughout the productive part of their working lives, they must have support upon release. It also behooves us as an agency to remember that we receive many wounded individuals. While structure is important, we also must provide warmth, concern and support if offenders are to begin healing.

The Rope

His peers described Lee as "not a mental heavyweight," but this did not keep him from being well liked by the other residents, black and white. They ignored his inattention to hygiene, a flaw they found insufferable in others. He had an enthusiastic interest in life they found appealing. At thirty-four, he still had managed to acquire and maintain a remarkably small amount of knowledge about the world. His lack of skills included the practical and the academic.

Lee was serious about religion, and he was serious about school. He worked frequently on fractions, his multiplication tables or other elementary math. His friends were willing to help. On several occasions, I observed other residents patiently drawing pie shapes and explaining fractions to Lee. Normally a quiet man, Lee did not stand out as someone who required additional help to accomplish daily tasks.

Lee could not remember to clock in and out when he finished his job assignments in the facility. Completely indigent, he counted on the $1.25 per day state inmates receive each month in state pay. When his pay arrived for the month, he found $11.25 in his envelope. His disappointment quickly turned to anger. Administrative Assistant Jane Sherer computed state pay and distributed the payments. Lee attempted to make her the object of his frustration.

Mrs. Sherer, with her shoulder-length, blond hair and 1960s skirts, did not look like a strong adversary. The years she spent as a nun and later as an air force non-commissioned officer were not revealed in her appearance. In short order, Lee received a clear lesson on the time clock and knowledge about his responsibility for his current cash shortage. About the time she finished her lecture, she realized Lee's disability.

A few weeks later, I found Lee and Mrs. Sherer in the basement. She was teaching him to paint. While far from professional, he was proudly accomplishing the task with reasonable competence.

November 5 was a stressful day. My office was cluttered with the remnants of a Halloween party. Christmas items for next month's events complicated the mess. Maintenance Supervisor Dave Dalton had completed a maintenance job, and plaster covered the clutter. I needed help — bad! I reviewed the status of residents who could be counted on to provide assistance. Seven residents were assigned to work in the center. Kerry and Rich were stripping wax from the cafeteria floor. Roger and Lonnie were doing a landscaping project at another center. Ted and Presley were in the middle of a painting project. No one was available…but Lee.

We started by separating items and placing them in storage boxes. We put Halloween makeup into plastic bags. We separated centerpieces into storable parts. Gradually, some order appeared in the room as the boxes were filled, marked and placed in the hall for relocation to the basement. In one corner of the room was a pile of nylon rope. I asked Lee to take out the tangles.

When he completed the task, I took one section of rope, grasped the end and looped the rope under my arm, over my shoulder and back through my hand, repeating this until I had a neat coil of rope. I took a strip of masking tape and secured the rope in the center for return to the tool closet. Lee looked at me with amazement. "You have done that before, haven't you?" I answered in the affirmative but did not understand his remark until I instructed him to do the same with another section.

He laid the rope on top of his shoulder and attempted to coil it. The rope fell off. This obviously would not work. I showed him how to secure the rope in his hand. He soon had the knack of it. A short while later, we finished the job and with a few recruits, took our carefully packed items to the basement to await another Halloween.

On my drive home, I thought about Lee and his skills. He did not win a vocational prize, earn his GED or land a $10-an-hour job. However, some of the very challenges that made it difficult for him to survive independently made him an excellent assistant. He was learning his multiplication tables, a little about responsibility, how to paint, and today he learned how to coil a rope. Somehow, it seemed just as important as the accomplishments of his more able peers, and I felt just as good.

The Face of a Rapist

For over an hour, I sat in a precinct police station in lower Manhattan looking at mug shots. I could clearly remember his black curly hair and green corduroy jacket, but the face from just an hour before would not come. Instead, I saw a blank oval. I had escaped, but the attack and attempted rape would not be easy to get past. For months, I would turn suddenly, thinking someone was following me and feel terror. For thirty-five years, the blank oval appeared each time I tried to remember the face. I could see the corduroy jacket and black curly hair in my dreams, but never the face. This incident and an even more painful crime committed against a member of my own family are important parts of a personal quest to reconcile advocacy for offenders with the needs of victims. I understand the temptation to want revenge.

I received a call from a reporter doing an upbeat story on recent honors given to St. Patrick for painting a mural and winning the City of Louisville Clean Block Contest. Contest preparation had taken two years of continuous work. The mural had taken six months to paint, and public relations with the businesses in our neighborhood could not have been better. The reporter questioned me about the projects, and then asked about the daily operations of the facility.

"What types of crimes have they committed?"

I discussed the pre-release residents (inmates), explained that they were in community custody and incarcerated for non-violent offenses. I also mentioned that parolees and halfway backs lived at the center. He asked again the nature of their charges. I responded that they could be any in the range of felony offenses. He continued to press. I more forcefully stated, "the range of felony offenses." He grew insistent. I declared that the information was not important for his story and the parole board had released them.

"It is important, and people will want to know," he insisted again.

Without releasing further information, I managed to extricate myself from the conversation. I waited several days for the news story to be released. I was anxious that the nature of the residents' offenses not overshadow what they had accomplished.

When it was published, the story was surprisingly upbeat. I was pleased to read about the accomplishments, hard work and commitment of the men of St. Patrick. When I finished, I remembered the reporter's last words to me, began to think about personal experiences, and related them to the crimes committed by the parolees and halfway backs. My thoughts gravitated to the only resident at St. Patrick charged with rape. I thought about Herman.

Herman was convicted and had been released from prison to parole. As the result of a technical parole violation, his parole officer later placed him in the halfway-back program at St. Patrick. Herman, a five-foot-nine white man with brown hair and eyes, was in his early thirties and worked in construction. He was married, had two children and a third on the way. He struggled in the many ways young married people struggle. The car broke down, the kids still needed transportation to day care, bills had to be paid and the lawn mowed.

Herman also struggled with his private demons. Sometimes his medication did not work and he fought against inappropriate thoughts. He went to a sex-offenders group, talked about his struggles, and his medication was adjusted. Substances were forbidden for serious reasons, as they could release his impulses. He regularly attended Alcoholics Anonymous and was sometimes a special speaker. The parole officer, sex-offender treatment staff and Dismas staff monitored Herman in his difficulties.

I worry much less about the sex offender in a community correctional center than I do about the one who lives in an ordinary neighborhood or goes to an ordinary school but has never been arrested. I have seen the face of a rapist many times. Although I have seen him too close in a back hallway and as an inmate in prison, I also have passed him, without knowledge, in a grocery store. His face does not stand out. He looks like any man on the street or even any teenager on a skateboard. In my case, his face has disappeared into a blank oval.

For every person in prison, somewhere there are victims. I have been one and so have members of my family. And there are other victims often harder to see. Sometimes, family members of the offenders are among the most devastated. Parents can spend a lifetime wondering what went wrong with their child. When an offender is convicted, his or her children grow up without this parent and sometimes are haunted by brutal events.

Despite my personal painful experiences with victims, I still believe the only reasonable justification for incarceration of an offender is to protect the public. Revenge seems only to enlarge the circle of victims. If revenge is not a satisfactory solution, then victims are left only with the gradual processing of grief and the search for understanding.

It is sometimes difficult to reconcile my work with offenders with my compassion for victims. Forgiveness sometimes seems beyond the reach of human ability. While it is difficult, I try to remember that an act is not a person. Although there are individuals with whom I could not deal fairly myself, I certainly hope that if intervention is required, the intervention will be restorative.

While there is humor in the daily life of working with offenders, it is a very serious and complicated business. It is a business that needs the best solutions we can develop, not our most primitive instincts, no matter how justified.

The Next Generation

When I reviewed six years of human interest stories for this collection, I selected very few from the earlier years. This is the only one I selected from 1995. It was originally untitled. The title came to me because I had knowledge of what happened over the next seven years. The young man involved in this story will be referred to as Rex in later pages. While most of the selections in this book have been edited to account for the passing years, I did not change this one.

Of French descent, Rex grew up in the rough, predominately white, inner-city neighborhood of Portland. With a mop of thick, curly black hair and a barrel chest, he was not significantly overweight, but his belt was on its last hole. He had a huge, childlike smile that could melt ice.

Rex lived at St. Patrick twice. After his first release, he quickly returned to drug abuse, and his parole was revoked. He wrote me several times from prison, begging to return. I wrote back and informed him that the Kentucky Department of Corrections classification system decides placement at a community correctional center, not the directors of individual centers. I also added that if he could arrange it with classification, I would be happy to have him. He returned to St. Patrick, stayed for over a year, and was again released to parole.

The grapevine kept me posted. Rex started using drugs again and was placed in residential treatment. For a while, he did well. He then returned to drugs and disappeared. He was on the run for a long time.

In January 2002, I received a letter from Rex. He was back in prison and wanted to return to St. Patrick. He told me that drugs had ruined his life and he was really through with them this time. This letter was not only similar to the ones I received several years before, but also to a conversation we had in 1995, after which I wrote a human interest story. I responded and told him I was retiring in a few weeks. I told him I hoped he could win his battle, and I sent a copy of this story:

(Dec. 6, 1995) Several weeks ago, a young man came into my office. We discussed crime, addiction and the Twelve-Step Program. We talked about his aunt. I had known her for many years. (She resided at Kentucky Correctional Institution for Women when I worked there.) He told me that she had now been drug-free for two years. Our conversation then turned to him.

The young man said he recently had cause to reevaluate the direction of his life. He has an eight-year-old son. Whenever he is not in prison, he always has assumed custody of his child. The two are very close. On a visit with the child, he told the boy that after his release he could live with him.

The boy replied excitedly, "Oh Daddy, you mean I can stay with you until the police come and get you again!"

St. Patrick in springtime

– PART TWO –

Day In, Day Out

When students interview correctional workers, they often ask them to describe a typical day — a difficult task, since no two days are the same. Individual needs interrupt long-range goals. Problems, critical and mundane, interrupt individual needs. Every day brings laughs. Many days bring tears. The subject matter in this section is as varied as a typical day.

Making a House a Home

St. Patrick dining room

Building design, décor and use of space set the stage for programming in a correctional facility. At the dedication of a new and beautiful prison building, one speaker commented, "We could have made it ugly at the same price." This seems an appropriate response to critics who are concerned when they perceive a correctional facility is "too nice" for offenders. In addition, these critics do not understand the connection between an attractive environment and positive behavior.

The large, stained-glass windows and high ceilings gave St. Patrick a natural beauty and a unique flavor. The challenge was to enhance the beauty and accommodate flaws that restricted programming. Eventually, an environment was developed that was conducive to healing the human spirit.

Informally evaluating the physical plant was one of the first tasks I completed upon becoming director. I immediately observed three cardboard boxes containing plastic eating utensils sitting on an ice machine as part of the serving line. The corners and edges of the floor were dirty throughout the building. A broken weight machine was crammed into the T.V. room, leaving no space in the only program area.

The basement looked like a dungeon. It was very damp, and mortar had fallen from between the bricks and lay in piles. Except for one set of shelves and massive amounts of junk on the floor, it appeared almost untouched since the church opened in 1862.

The living areas were disorganized. Without space to organize their belongings, residents spread things everywhere and set their televisions in folding chairs. The paved backyard was bare except for three wooden picnic tables. The sun literally baked the area. The residents appeared generally hostile and had no investment in their surroundings.

The first priority seemed to be a thorough cleaning of the facility. The first major purchase was a serving table and containers for the plastic eating utensils. Another priority was to move the weight equipment out of the TV room so residents had an area for Alcoholics Anonymous meetings and recreation. Beach umbrellas added to the backyard made it conducive to activities. Nightstands and top bunk shelves were added to the living areas.

As the center became more comfortable, residents began proposing their own ideas for improvement. They readily gave their labor to accomplish these ideas.

The basement was tuck-pointed and painted. Shelves were added. A dehumidifier soon removed the excess moisture. Furniture in the cafeteria was replaced. Plants and pictures were added. Fresh coats of paint were applied. The exercise equipment was upgraded. The residents raised money in a car wash to replace the TV room carpet. A dishwasher was purchased, and paper plates and plastic utensils were replaced with real dishes and silverware. Seasonal decorations were purchased. Flowers, chairs and a cat were added to the backyard.

Slowly and steadily, the center changed in appearance. With these changes came attitude changes in the residents. While most days brought new problems, the atmosphere improved and investment in the center increased.

Soon, former staff and residents were coming back to visit. They brought stories of new jobs, successes, problems and new babies. They brought news of others, sometimes of those not so successful. These visits were homecomings. I believe that together, we made a house a home.

The Rat

One morning, along with catalogs, bills, complaints and forms, the director's mailbox contained the following dispatch:

Ms. Chandler, This is Job I was playing with the Rat scaring people and it got riped I dont no if I am the one who riped it but I fixed it. Job. (sic)

I taped the note above my desk and smiled. The rat in question, a stuffed Halloween decoration about two feet tall, was found on top of the living area trashcan with minor damage. An unnamed resident, assuming the damage was vandalism, reported the mangled rat and gave me the names of the culprits.

Upon investigation, I learned that one of the younger residents had put the rat in a friend's bed and from there it became a football. Having once been twenty years old myself (I thought back to the day the dean's bicycle was found hanging from the Berea College water tower), I understood the attraction of practical jokes. I substituted amusement for anger about the incident. The informal information system at St. Patrick had worked again, and a little mystery had been solved.

Novice correctional employees must come to terms early in their careers with two ethical issues, the use of informants and the use of power. Inmates will test the novice on these concepts quickly, and the novice must be prepared. Offenders will re-administer the tests each time the employee changes locations.

Warden John Bill Dotson, my first correctional mentor, advised me not to buy information with favors. He explained that purchased information is unreliable, and the motives of the informant are questionable. I used his advice through the years when inmates offered me information for favors.

I always gave the same response: "I do not give favors for information. If you feel that it is in the best interest of this population for me to have the information, I would appreciate it. However, there can be no payment."

The resident would walk out the door. I would wait. I could almost hear the sneakers squeak on the floor as the informant turned around and a short time later told me what was on his mind. I evaluated the truthfulness and motivation of the informant and seldom used the information immediately unless it was critical and had been corroborated by other sources. I stored it in the back of my mind until it fit together with other data to solve a puzzle.

The inmate ethic of not informing the authorities, of not being a "rat," promotes unlawful activity and violence. The larger and harsher the correctional environment, the more pervasive is this ethic. In large prisons especially, inmate bullies use this ethic to their advantage and mistreat weaker inmates with little fear of reprisal. Seldom do inmates and even staff examine this ethic. They often react with shock when it is questioned.

One day I heard a resident tell others in the backyard that a "rat" was the most despicable human being in existence.

I posed this question. "Are you telling me that if an inmate stabs someone and takes his belongings, a person who reports this to employees paid to safeguard inmates is worse than the bully who steals, stabs or even worse? Somehow this does not make much sense to me."

The resident scratched his head. It had not occurred to him.

When offenders are intent on blaming a "rat," they sometimes blame other residents even when staff resolves an investigation by other means. At Kentucky Correctional Institution for Women, my office was adjacent to an inmate bathroom and down the hall from an inmate lounge. When marijuana smoke wafted into my office from the direction of the bathroom, I sent a correctional officer into the lounge to write down the names of the inmates in the lounge. Upon leaving for the evening, I gave the list to the night shift and requested they perform urine drops on those listed. Nine screens out of eleven tested positive for marijuana A brawl occurred in one of the dormitories when the inmates began accusing each other of being "rats."

As a control device, offenders sometimes accuse those they perceive as weak of being "rats" but seldom accuse the strong, even if they have cause. Strong residents occasionally even tell others, "I am not taking a fall for you. If you do it again, I'll report you." Other residents do not dare call them rats, and generally, this stops the offensive activity. In my experience, the stronger residents, not the timid ones, made the most reports on others.

The issue of "rats" naturally leads to the issue of power. Inmates respect confidence, and they sometimes confuse kindness with weakness. I remember the unorthodox response Warden Dotson gave me when I approached him with a problem of an inmate invading my personal space. I explained that the man did not touch me or say anything inappropriate — he just leaned too close and he did this frequently. I told him my plan to talk with the man in my office.

"Don't do it. Get him in public with a group of other inmates. Say something to embarrass him. He won't violate your space anymore."

I followed instructions and passed my first test in power and one-upmanship. From then on, the inmate left me alone. He murdered a jail chaplain a few years later, so apparently, I was right in feeling uneasy.

My first real test by residents at St. Patrick came about two months after arrival. Between April and September of 1995, three different administrators consecutively occupied the director's office. As in any period of instability, tension became the norm, and offenders with their power preoccupation tested the limits. Initially, the incident did not appear to be a test or even an internal problem.

Resident Monitor Jimmy Overton worked on the evening shift. At about 6:30 p.m., he went to his car, parked on Thirteenth Street near the back entrance of the facility, to retrieve his supper. Appalled at what he found, he immediately returned to the center and reported someone had bashed in the front windshield of his car. A large club lay near the car. We discussed the incident and concluded neighborhood vandals were responsible. Mr. Overton, a seminary student on a limited budget, did not have collision insurance and had no idea how he could afford the necessary repair. It did not occur to any of us that the vandalism came from within until the next morning.

The residents knew and they talked. By 10 a.m., we had put together the various reports made to staff members and concluded the following. A parolee, Pete, frequently violated the facility rule limiting phone calls to ten minutes during peak hours. Mr. Overton ordered Pete off the phone. The next evening, Pete and Paul, another parolee, smashed the window. As I did not have all the information needed, I ordered the parolees placed on restriction for purposes of investigation and asked staff to inform the men when they returned from work. Since parolees have considerable freedom and a restriction stings, it came as no surprise when the two culprits came to see me.

They stormed into my office demanding to know the reason for the restriction. An Academy Award would have been appropriate for the act that followed as they proclaimed innocence and indignation. I told them firmly that they were under investigation for breaking Mr. Overton's car window. They asked the duration of the restriction.

"Until the investigation is complete." Given my state of mind at the time, I also may have mentioned something about the weather in hell.

I took statements from a number of staff and residents during the next day. I determined that the window was broken at approximately 6 p.m. and that Pete and Paul returned to the center at 5:30 p.m. The chain of events became clear in my mind. I called Pete in for a private interview.

"Paul and I were in the center at 5:30 the night the window got broke, we couldn't have done it."

"You and Paul went out the back door for a smoke break, and when the staff member wasn't looking, you slipped out through the driveway to Thirteenth Street, broke the window and returned without being missed."

"You have it on tape, don't you?"

I held my cards tight. I made it a policy not to lie to residents, but a bluff seemed appropriate at this point. "That's a security issue and I can't discuss it."

"What if Paul and I agreed to pay for the window?"

"You mean like an Alford plea?" (A legal defendant can use an Alford plea in lieu of a guilty or innocent plea to acknowledge that, while not admitting guilt, there is enough information to find him guilty.)

"Yeah."

"Let me talk to Paul and your parole officer. I'll let you know."

I talked to the parole officers for both men and explained that, while I knew they broke the window and a vision of the two in hand-cuffs did not make me unhappy, my information would not stand up in a parole revocation hearing. I wanted the car window repaired. We agreed that I would document the incident on a disciplinary report, and if the men gave an Alford plea, paying for the window would be an appropriate punishment. And that was the way it happened.

This event became a turning point for the center. The residents of St. Patrick committed no other acts of vandalism in the local community. They became, in fact, good neighbors and sentinels. On several occasions, they locked padlocks on the gates of nearby businesses left open by careless employees, and twice they reported burglaries in progress. The reports resulted in calls to the police and led to arrests.

If I had any doubts about the guilt of Pete and Paul, it was resolved when I read Pete's evaluation form at the end of his stay. The residents completed the forms in confidence, and unless the resident elected to sign his name, the identity was secret. Pete signed his name, and on a one-to-five scale, with five being the best, he rated St. Patrick five in every area.

While residents test limits, they feel safer if staff passes the test. Residents are very realistic, and they fear their peers in an atmosphere without control more than they fear reprisals from staff. Inmates fear chaos even if they are the ones creating it. They want staff to enforce rules, but like all of us, they do not want to be insulted or humiliated. The ideal staff member is a smiling cop, someone who enforces rules but does so in a diplomatic fashion.

Through the years at St. Patrick, staff generally gained information about the infractions important to center security. Residents assured this by either telling a staff member or telling another resident who would. The information made me a more effective director. When residents gave me information, I respected this trust, recognizing that without it, the safety of staff and residents could be in jeopardy. When residents questioned me about how I obtained information, I responded with a cliché, "Mother knows all." Or "The walls talk." Or "I just know."

PART TWO – *Day In, Day Out*

What Is a Community?

Sunflowers on Market Street

In August 1995, the St. Patrick community extended from the front gate to the back door. The neighborhood was seen as a hostile environment. Most of the neighboring businesses viewed the arrival of a community correctional center with suspicion. There were many homeless and desperate people on the trash-strewn streets, and cars were broken into regularly. A few months before my arrival, someone broke into St. Patrick through the window and left by the same route. Staff found blood on the windowsill.

The first major request I made was for a backyard gate. Primarily, I wanted to keep the neighborhood and contraband out and improve accountability for our residents. A recent incident of two parolees slipping out the back drive and vandalizing a staff vehicle illustrated the need for this accountability. Just as important for center security was the need to change the atmosphere.

When I worked for the corrections department, I frequently talked with inmates returning from jail-release programs. The most common complaint was, "We were locked in, and we could not go outside." The center required inmates to stay inside with hourly smoke breaks supervised by staff. We had a choice: Permit residents to go on the backyard and deal with security problems, or supervise hourly smoke breaks.

Supervised smoke breaks tied up the staff, and when the staff forgot breaks during busy periods, residents became angry. I believed any system of rules that pits staff against residents and administration against staff should be reviewed. We got the gate and were able to keep the yard open from 5 a.m. to 10 p.m. daily. Our neighborhood expanded to the backyard. That gate was the single best investment made for the operation of the facility.

A visiting Kentucky official, Mary Beth Schmidt, and an inmate, Roger, next required me to review my concept of neighborhood. Ms. Schmidt visited the center once and slipped on crab apples that fell from our tree onto the city sidewalk. She requested rather strongly that these be removed. Roger wanted to clean up under the viaduct, a block away. It is all history now, but our neighborhood gradually expanded to include seven city blocks.

As residents picked up trash, swept and landscaped areas, we made friends. We loaned and borrowed. Businesses became advocates. We communicated. We helped each other. Relationships with businesses grew steadily more productive. One business, an archenemy in 1995, wrote a letter of support in 1996. The bonds to build this relationship were forged by our daily cleanups, communication and cooperation.

In 1997 and 1998, St. Patrick, in conjunction with the East Russell Neighborhood Association and local businesses, organized a neighborhood cleanup. Beecher Terrace, a nearby public housing development, held a breakfast for the men from St. Patrick, local businesses and public housing to kick off the cleanup. This consortium of volunteers cleaned the entire sixty blocks of the neighborhood in one day!

The next problem challenging us was the number of homeless people in the immediate neighborhood. We dealt with homelessness in a variety of ways. While homeless people came to understand that hobo beds in the nearby bushes would not be tolerated, we recognized them as a part of our community. We frequently gave them leftover food, water, coffee or directions. Sometimes we called The Healing Place, a local drug rehab center, to have them transported to safety and treatment. On a frigid winter day, Luke found a homeless man behind a dumpster covered in snow and crying. The resident monitor on duty called an ambulance. The medical technician found the man within an hour of death. When the hospital released him, he went to The Healing Place. While the homeless people seldom returned favors, other neighbors did.

Luke asked me to pick up some dry beans and fatback for the men to cook for lunch. I did not get around to doing it. A week later, a neighborhood community center called to ask for help moving a piano. Some St. Patrick residents moved the piano, and I left the community center with their token of thanks — two bags of beans.

In 1999, Molly Leonard, a leader of the nearby Portland community, asked the residents of St. Patrick to paint the viaduct at Twenty-Ninth Street and Portland Avenue. The Toll Bridge Inn, a Portland restaurant, volunteered to give the workers free lunch. The crew ate lunch at the Toll Bridge for almost a week. "Miss Molly," a white, retired city employee in her sixties made friends with the young, black artist, Reggie. All residents were mannerly, polite and personable. The bonds forged that week were to pay unexpected and incredible dividends two years later in the Portland neighborhood.

Because of overcrowding in the local jail, Dismas Charities was on contract for many years with Jefferson County to care for county offenders. These misdemeanor offenders lived in Dismas Charities Portland, in the Portland community of Louisville. A new jail opened and the contract ceased. At a zoning board hearing in February 2001, Dismas Charities Inc. requested to house state inmates — felons — in the empty facility. Although the Portland community had strongly protested the original opening of Dismas Charities Portland and the issue had potential for great controversy, this time the reaction was quite different.

Businesses in the St. Patrick neighborhood sent letters of testimony. Molly Leonard, a powerful influence in Portland, and Herb Broderick, owner of the Toll Bridge (and president of the Portland Business Association), stepped forward and testified for Dismas. Not one person came forward to protest reopening the Portland facility for felons.

Our success in changing the character of the neighborhood brought other recognition in 2001. Our alderman, George Unseld, honored our neighboring businesses and St. Patrick with a luncheon. Alderman Unseld gave Luke and the custodian of the nearby Lutheran church special recognition for their work in cleaning the neighboring streets. The recognition to this little neighborhood was especially significant because of the nature of the population — light industry, the homeless, one church, a liquor store and sixty felons in the middle of the inner city. The sixty felons were the catalysts of the miraculous change.

I believe it is important for directors of community correctional centers to understand the importance of forging bonds in the community. Dividends can come years later at zoning hearings or immediately with a bag of beans. For better or worse, our centers and our residents are part of the community. It is up to us to define the nature of the relationship.

Main Street viaduct (before)

Main Street viaduct (after)

The Day I Set the Toilet on Fire
or
The Perversity of Inanimate Objects

When asking questions about my career, others sometimes expressed sympathy for what they perceived as a difficult job. They seemed to think the primary challenge was with the residents. Although disagreeing, I did not correct them. Actually, the Number One challenge was staff, followed by inanimate objects. Residents were a distant third. In this story, I will explore the perversity of those inanimate objects.

A stained-glass window came loose. An expert examined the window and submitted a bid for repair. On the day Dismas Chief Executive Officer Ray Weis approved the bid, the window fell, breaking into countless pieces and causing us to obtain a new (and more expensive) bid. For genuine perversity, however, stained glass does not hold a candle to plumbing.

In 1997, on the day of our annual Halloween extravaganza, the sink elected to become hopelessly clogged. A great dose of drain cleaner resulted only in a terrible smell. While the maintenance department came to the rescue, the odor lingered well into the evening.

The weather turned bitterly cold, and Maintenance Supervisor Dave Dalton turned on the heat. Only two of the three heaters worked, resulting in a great cry of anguish from the resident population. Staff and residents wore coats around the clock, and nerves were on edge. The tension reached a peak one chilly day when I followed Mr. Dalton to the basement, where we screamed at each other in frustration.

Mr. Dalton drained the boilers, set the thermostat to compensate for the missing heater and called in a heating company. The company determined that the part needed to repair the heater could not be located within the city limits and was on a three-week backorder. As soon as Mr. Dalton drained the boiler, the dishwasher water temperature mysteriously dropped by ten degrees, causing a sanitation problem. A few days later, the outside temperature went up again, which caused the adjusted thermostat to produced a heat wave, resulting in another great cry of anguish.

And on November 19, 1997, I set the toilet on fire. It had been a difficult day. A resident returned late from work, was declared absconded, and before staff could gather up his clothing, a few members of the population decided to relieve him of his valuables. I was livid. Not only did they steal his coat, shoes and hat, but they took his underwear! A locker shakedown netted some of his belongings in a vacant locker and revealed the dirty conditions of the other lockers. As rage is not my normal state, I tried to hold on to the anger, planning to vent it dramatically in the November 20 population meeting.

Setting the toilet on fire almost took away the finely tuned hostility. The task was to learn how to deactivate one smoke detector while keeping the others operational. In order to practice, a detector had to be activated then put out of commission. Assistant Director Kathlene Bello suggested that someone stand on a chair and blow smoke into a detector.

"Oh no" I said. "That will cause the building to smell like cigarette smoke."

I, as the boss, had a better idea. I rolled up a piece of newspaper and went into the staff bathroom. I lit the newspaper. The detector would not go off. The newspaper kept burning, so I threw it into the commode. Immediately, flames engulfed the toilet cover. I flushed, but the toilet kept burning. When the fire was finally extinguished, the bottom of the toilet cover was black. The resident janitor was summoned. It took considerable effort to remove the ashes, and it took sandpaper to repair the cover. My dignity was not so easily recovered.

Assistant Director Bello directed someone to blow smoke into a detector. This worked — proving, of course, that the boss is not always right.

Later, I regained some of my righteous anger. The population was properly chastised. The property was returned. The lockers were cleaned.

The inanimate objects did not respond so well. The next day, St. Patrick had a leaking sink, malfunctioning locks, cove base collapse and, of course, a toilet lid with a large black scar.

Stained-glass window
at St. Patrick

Men's Tears

On the right side of my desk at St. Patrick, I kept a box of tissues. I learned long ago that tissues were an essential tool of the trade. While useful for sniffles and spills, the tissues were really there to capture the tears of men. I would like to share three of their stories.

Oliver, at six foot four inches with long arms, bone-thin legs and poor posture, appeared to be all angles. At forty-six, his countenance was much like a black version of Abe Lincoln. Oliver walked off from parole years ago, but instead of continuing in criminal behavior, he changed his lifestyle. He worked, later married and maintained a loving relationship with his wife.

Oliver's wife developed terminal breast cancer, and as he was struggling through the most difficult time of his life, his past finally caught up with him. Located by the law, he was taken into custody and returned to prison. Later, he was transferred to St. Patrick. As he discussed her illness and the pain of separation, he burst into anguished and guilty tears. I could only listen.

With medium build and sandy-blond hair only a month or so over-due for a trim, Carl did not appear to have severe emotional problems. Only the stress wrinkles on his forehead and the strangeness in his light blue eyes gave hints of his inner turmoil. Prior to paroling to St. Patrick, he lived in a special unit at Kentucky State Reformatory (KSR), where his medication was monitored. After arriving at the center, he stopped medication and avoided making an appointment with a mental health clinic. The consequences of this medication lapse were not long in coming.

One evening, Carl provoked busy staff with a demand that they immediately give him the dinner that had been saved for him. He then made a scene and received a disciplinary report. Next, he burst into my office and demanded return to prison. I said that I could certainly accommodate him and indicated I would call his parole officer. I picked up the phone but didn't complete the call. We started talking.

Carl talked about the saved meal and his overreaction. We talked about medication and why he was trying to avoid it. We talked about KSR, the smells, the walls and the staff. He burst into tears of embarrassment. After drying his eyes, he admitted that he really didn't want to return to prison. After Carl left the office, he met with his counselor, who arranged for a clinic appointment. Carl resumed medication, gradually learned to share his frustrations with selected staff, and his angry outbursts ceased.

Reggie found it natural to talk with me when he had problems. At KSR, he worked in the barbershop, a department under my administrative jurisdiction. When he arrived at St. Patrick, he became the center artist for a community service project I coordinated. In our lives before prison, he had been a sailor and I had been a marine. Before the many years of drug addiction ravaged his resume, he had an excellent start on life. Short and muscular, with brown skin and close-cropped hair, he was a leader within the inmate population.

Reggie's mother was in the hospital with a stroke and multiple medical problems. We talked, and I suggested we try to get permission for an emergency furlough or a visit. He wanted this and clearly understood a bedside visit would eliminate the possibility of going to her funeral, should she pass away. His counselor called the hospital, but the nurse's assessment did not include immediate death. We could proceed no further, as the supervising authority's position on this matter was very clear: Bedside visits only were approved in cases where death seemed imminent.

Reggie became furious with me, feeling that somehow I should be able to arrange the visit. He told his counselor he was withdrawing from all center activities. I did not appreciate his attitude or his attempt to punish me by this immature method. Still, he needed to see his mother.

I requested the counselor make a follow-up call to the doctor for more information. With new information, the counselor contacted the parole officer, and he approved an unescorted visit. Reggie requested that his counselor accompany him and stay at the hospital. Upon arrival, they found his mother tethered by tubes. She barely recognized him and could scarcely talk. At her bedside, he burst into racking tears and could stay only a short time. When Reggie returned to the center, he came to talk to me. We talked about his grief, his anger and my anger. He cried, and I handed out tissues.

Amid the many chores that consume a director — purchasing, completing the cursed monthly director's report, auditing files, programming, staffing, fixing broken toilets, attending meetings — it was easy to forget what was truly important. As I wrote about these men, other tasks fell into proper perspective. All too frequently, we forget the common bonds we have with the incarcerated and fail to see the tears.

Courage and Honesty

The St. Patrick resident floor specialist, Kerry, requested a stripping buffer. When residents made reasonable requests for equipment that would improve the center's operation or appearance, every effort was made to accommodate them. This was especially true of Kerry, whose dedication and creativity were truly remarkable. I explained that a stripping buffer was expensive and the possibility of acquiring one was remote, but I was willing to try.

Maintenance Supervisor Dave Dalton came by a few days later, and I asked him if there was a stripping buffer around anywhere. (It was a long shot, as most centers have high-speed buffers.) He told me that the Lexington center had one they were not using and promised to bring it when he made his next trip to Lexington. Good as his word, the buffer arrived a few weeks later.

In the meantime, Kerry learned to use the high-speed buffer for stripping and found the newly arrived stripping buffer to be useless. Residents and staff moved it from place to place to get it out of the way. Sometime during the summer, we began preparations for a special guest. In order to further enhance the appearance of St. Patrick, a staff member who shall remain nameless directed that the buffer be put outside in the fenced dumpster area for temporary storage.

Apparently, this unnamed staff member forgot the buffer. A month or so later, I discovered the buffer in the rain. Appalled, I fussed and stomped around and then became distracted. I forgot it. The abuse of the buffer continued, and it remained out in the weather.

I now must digress from the negligence of staff to the misconduct of a resident. Some residents bring special talents to a corrections setting. If the talent is combined with personality and time in the center, these residents come closer to the inner circle of influence. In many ways, through their ideas and their work, they become very valuable. When such residents are involved in major transgressions, the impact on the center, the other residents and the staff is stronger. Reggie was such a resident. He was the primary artist on the summer community project and made many contributions through his art. A secondary job as center barber made him indispensable to the well-groomed. Other residents respected Reggie, and staff had high expectations of him.

Reggie made a big mistake, and he lied about it. Assistant Director Kathlene Bello conducted an investigation and issued Reggie a disciplinary report. The proof was positive and when confronted with the evidence, he finally confessed. (Lying when afraid was an adaptive behavior for him.) Reggie was terrified and convinced that the parole officers were coming to take him away in handcuffs any minute. Instead, he had a disciplinary hearing.

I was the obvious person to chair Reggie's disciplinary hearing. Getting his attention had obviously already been accomplished, but turning a bad experience into a therapeutic intervention was the challenge of the disciplinary hearing committee. The committee opted to restrict him from the telephone (his favorite activity) for twenty days and require him to write an essay on the relationship between courage and honesty. The committee told him not to turn in the essay for fifteen days so he could think about it. The essay was well done and very honest. After the experience, we frequently discussed the concepts and the value of this experience in changing his thinking.

Now I will return to Mr. Dalton and the buffer. In late December, I saw the buffer again, still out in the weather. I was very disgusted with myself. I had failed to care for an expensive piece of equipment that I personally had requested. That morning I saw Mr. Dalton and told him that we did not use the buffer and asked him to take it to the Dismas storage area. He agreed and said he could bring his truck to the back door and get it.

"Oh no!" I said. "We will carry it up front for you."

Reggie and several other residents were observing my discomfort.

Reggie said, "Courage and honesty, Mrs. Chandler, courage and honesty."

"Just where," asked Mr. Dalton, catching on, "is the buffer stored?"

There in front of them all, I confessed....

Daffodils in traffic island
Tweedledum and Tweedledee handiwork

Tweedledum and Tweedledee

Tweedledum and Tweedledee

Agreed to have a battle;

For Tweedledum said Tweedledee

Had spoiled his nice new rattle.

— Lewis Carroll

The master of one-upmanship at St. Patrick was a man named Wilson. His family came from the same section of Eastern Kentucky as the more rowdy side of my family. There was likely a genetic kinship. His ability to con others into doing as he wished was both unsettling and familiar to me.

I received Wilson in trade from the director of another center. (We both thought we were getting the better end of the deal.) When Wilson arrived, I had problems finding a community service placement for him. Staff at the other center had disciplined Wilson for not being on site; consequently, this eliminated solo travel and several job work placements. After several calls, I finally found Wilson and another equally problematic resident placements working for a city maintenance department.

Three weeks later, I received a call from the maintenance director. "These two men you sent me are too strong for my supervisor. He can't handle them."

The city maintenance director wanted to temporarily disband the crew and start over in a month or so, minus Wilson. I complied.

A dishwashing position at St. Patrick was open, and this seemed like a perfect new assignment for Wilson. Wilson quickly got tired of this job, and some days he smoothly avoided work by convincing other residents that they needed to share his experience. He even recruited a replacement (whom I vetoed). I heard on the grapevine that he was paying $5 for washing the dinner dishes. It seemed that every day someone had a new Wilson joke about his unique skills to get others to share in dishwashing.

As the result of another disciplinary report, Wilson managed to acquire forty hours of extra duty in addition to his dishwashing tasks. The mechanical room, off the beaten track and including the emergency exit from the second floor, needed painting. Believing nothing should be wasted, I thought some obscenely bright blue paint taking up space in the basement and Wilson's dubious skills seemed to fill the bill. The mess he quickly created became an item of discussion for the entire center. Muttering and sputtering, the center painter, Phillip, finally ordered Wilson out of the room. Phillip cursed and painted for three days until the area became attractive and cheerful. Wilson neither volunteered nor was invited to join the ongoing special work crews that fall.

I assigned Phillip, Reggie and Kevin to raking the traffic island on Thirteenth Street in preparation for planting daffodil bulbs. All three men were extremely hard workers. Phillip and Reggie were convinced that they knew best how to tackle almost anything. Phillip's brain and mouth seemed one and the same, and he always said exactly what was on his mind without considering the impact on others. Reggie was very sensitive to criticism, and his relationship with Phillip was naturally problematic. Shortly after sending them to the job, I got in my car and headed out for lunch.

Reggie hailed me, came to my car window and said he was going to hit Phillip with a shovel. He explained that Phillip wanted to edge around the inside of the island, which would take "forever," and

Kevin needed the cart for trash. I got out of my car and told Kevin to keep the cart on site. I told Reggie that edging the island was a good idea, and I got back in my car to go to lunch.

At Fifteenth Street, it occurred to me that Reggie had threatened to hit Phillip with a shovel. I turned around and came back to the traffic island. Phillip and Reggie were working — Phillip was edging, Reggie was raking, and the cart was on site. When I inquired about the legitimate use of shovels, they both laughed and assured me all was safe. I went to lunch. They completed the job with no mayhem.

Another source of conflict at St. Patrick was a feud between those who believed items should be saved for any possible use and those who believed that unused items should be trashed. I am a saver. Administrative Assistant Jane Sherer was a tosser. Reggie was in her club. Mrs. Sherer, Reggie and associates were cleaning out the basement. I came into the backyard, near the entrance to the basement. Reggie warned me to stay away. With fear and trembling, I complied.

A day or so later, I needed a paint color sample for the paint salesman. I could not find the sample card, but I recalled that we threw the bucket with the correct color in the trash. With some assistance, I proceeded to examine the contents of the dumpster. I found, not only the bucket, but a perfectly good chair with the seat broken. I knew we could replace the board and have a good chair. I had it pulled out of the trash and went looking for Reggie.

"Wilson knows about it," he said. "Why are you asking me?"

I told him that I was certain he knew something about it, and he did. It turned out that Wilson had stood on the chair, the board had broken, and Mrs. Sherer directed him to put it in the trash.

A few days later, I went looking for the crutches we usually kept on hand. In the smoke tent, I found Reggie, Wilson and a collection of other jokesters. I told Reggie the crutches were not in the basement and wanted to know if he put them in the trash. He assured me that the crutches were safe. Realizing that he was going to be leaving soon, I asked who I was going to blame for things when he left.

He pointed, and the group said in unison, "Wilson!"

Stress and anxiety frequently accompanied me on the hour commute home in the evening. On other days, I felt rewarded. That evening, I thought about the daily bantering and smiled all the way home.

The Fox and the Hound
or
The Law of Supply and Demand

One night I came home from work and found a gift on the dining room table. The gift gave me cause to celebrate both a career that was drawing toward an end and the unusual people I had met along the way. I smiled and remembered a day over twenty years before when I met a particularly competent practitioner of prison commerce. It also gave me cause to review some other enterprising individuals I met along the way.

Commerce exists in every form wherever human beings are gathered. The law of supply and demand and the need to support oneself seem to be basic human drives. Years of repressive governments and even incarceration have not been able to eliminate these impulses. I gradually learned about correctional commerce as I journeyed through employment at two Kentucky minimum-security facilities,

Kentucky Correctional Institution for Women (KCIW) and Kentucky State Reformatory (KSR) and finally to St. Patrick.

Unauthorized movement of property and commerce within correctional facilities must be understood, not in black and white, but in shades of gray. At the harmless end of the spectrum is the gift to someone who does not have something from the one who does. Correctional inmates frequently share cigarettes or go through their property to give to those who have little.

Two best friends, inmates at KCIW, went to the prison canteen together. One had money on her account and the other did not. The prosperous inmate bought two ice cream cones and handed one to her friend. The correctional officer supervising the canteen line knew the inmate rulebook thoroughly and enforced every rule: "No gifts, no borrowing and no lending." At that time, I presided over the KCIW disciplinary committee and had to deal with the resulting disciplinary report. The inmates had broken a rule. I tried hard not to roll my eyes as I handed out a warning.

The next level of prison commerce is sales of goods and services — making beds, repairing broken items and running stores. Inmates frequently utilize paid facility jobs for personal profit. Most common are legal services, barbers and laundry jobs. In milder cases, extra services receive tips.

As deputy warden for programs at KSR, one of my responsibilities was to assure supervision of the inmate barbershop. With interest, I investigated the unauthorized payments the inmate barbers were alleged to receive. It was almost a lost cause. I tracked down numerous tips on how the payments, packs of cigarettes, were passed to the barber. I shook down the barbershop repeatedly but in vain. I never could find the payments or a clue to how they were transferred.

Four years later, I found the answer. One of the KSR barbers I knew, Reggie, came to St. Patrick. He was assigned to be the St. Patrick barber shortly after arrival. We had a number of conversations about honesty during his stay. The day he paroled and was leaving St. Patrick, I had some questions for him.

"At the KSR barbershop, how were the payments made, and where did they put the cigarettes?"

He asked if I remembered the stack of mattresses by the door of the clothing house just in front of the barbershop. I did.

"They were slipped between the mattresses."

"And how much did you charge for haircuts at St. Patrick?"

"How do you know I was charging?"

"I just know," I answered.

"Two dollars," he replied.

In the worst-case scenarios, prison commerce has real victims. Inmates who cannot pay are deprived of essential services. Clothing, for example, may be ruined by sabotage if the client does not pay the laundry man. The inmates do not report the abuse because of the prevailing institutional ethic that discourages reporting to the authorities. A prison black market sometimes exists in drugs, alcohol, sex or violence. Prison commerce may even reach out and include victims in the public.

Allison sat in a prison dormitory at KCIW and made $50,000. Long blond hair and clear classic features gave her an edge. Her con was the "Dear Sweetie Pie Letter." The scam begins with the placement of an ad in a personal column, portraying a lonely young woman who has been mistreated by society. The inmate sends to the mark a photograph of a beautiful woman, usually purchased from another inmate. (Allison used her own picture and made extra bucks by selling her photograph to other women who had the same verbal skills but not the same looks.) The first few letters discuss the desire for long walks and candlelit dinners. Then come statements about the need for medical treatment or education, but the lack of financial means. The next request is for money to pay a fine to get out of prison. Lastly, about the time the resident makes parole, the victim is told to send money to buy a plane ticket.

Allison played the game well and had seven or eight paying customers sending plane fare just before she was scheduled to leave. She did not leave as planned. Some determined work on the part of the staff located two victims who agreed to prosecute. Allison found herself doing another two years.

I again looked at the gift on my table and recalled how I met the donor through an American Correctional Association (ACA) mock audit. During my tenure with the Department of Corrections, the ACA accredited all Kentucky Department of Corrections adult institutions. The accreditation process is very involved, and prisons usually have mock audits performed by staff of other institutions to help ensure the facility is ready.

Sometime in the 1980s, while I was deputy warden at KCIW, I was dispatched to Kentucky State Reformatory to assist with a mock audit. The KSR administrative staff assigned Warden Steve Smith from another institution and me to the kitchen. We were very thorough, reviewing every food service standard.

In the basement of the kitchen was a maintenance shop. In the shop were three inmates and numerous large wooden storage cabinets. My hound's instinct told me several things:

1. Inmates seldom hide contraband in their living area; the work area is more common.

2. Inmates who work maintenance are frequently privileged characters, valuable to staff and not given the scrutiny other inmates are given.

3. What a great hiding place!

What happened next is as accurate as I can make it, given all the years that have passed. I looked at an inmate with mounds of long, red hair and said, "Open that drawer."

With hesitation, he complied. We knew immediately what we had found…the KSR radio repair shop! In the drawer, and several others, were countless portable radios in various states of disassembly. There were hundreds of ear pads, broken earphones, circuit boards and rolls of electrical tape.

We could have called internal affairs. We could have issued a disciplinary report. The penalty of a disciplinary report for the entrepreneurs was a probable ninety days in segregation (also known as the hole). The creativity and humor of the operation, so in the open, struck us as funny, but we did not laugh. I looked over my glasses at the man I will call "The Fox."

"When you get your radio repair certification, send me a copy. And…clean up this mess."

The next day, the shop was gone.

Seventeen or eighteen years later, my husband met "The Fox" many miles from KSR and under different circumstances. "The Fox," long released, was an active member of Alcoholics Anonymous and was caring for his 80-year-old mother. Their discussion of prison life and my husband's last name brought to light the story and his gratitude for not ending up in the hole. After acquiring a hard-earned vocational certification, he had it framed and sent it to me along with a note thanking me for caring. It was now sitting on my dining room table.

In our countless contacts with offenders, corrections professionals seldom know the seeds they sow. In this case, I know. The framed certificate went on my wall, to be treasured forever. I sent a copy of this story to "The Fox" to let him know how much the certificate means to me, a reminder of the struggles offenders have during and after incarceration and the contributions they can make to society when they succeed. Men like "The Fox" validate commitment to the dignity and worth of all human beings.

cc: The Fox

Bud Makes Parole

Bud, the St. Patrick cat

In September 1998, I went on vacation. When I left, the center had fifty-five residents and a tomcat named AJ. AJ, named for a staff member, Resident Monitor Albert Russell, was an integral part of the St. Patrick social scene. When I returned to St. Patrick, I found fifty-five residents, AJ and Bud.

Bud, gray, handsome and proud, appeared to be a neutered tomcat and was thoroughly enmeshed in the fabric of the center. Secretly, I thought two cats were one cat too many, but I held a minority opinion. I admitted defeat and Bud stayed.

While I know that animals require responsible medical care, I reasoned that if Bud was neutered, he had shots. I postponed a veterinary appointment. This was a mistake. Bud jumped into the lap of an unsuspecting resident, and his claw pierced the man's pants, giving him a small scratch on the leg. Ever practical and resourceful, Counselor Brigid Adams called the health department for advice regarding tetanus shot requirements.

At once, the woman at the health department said since we had no proof of rabies shots, Bud must be picked up and housed at St. Patrick's expense for ten days. The woman kept calling the scratch a bite. Other calls to vets received the interpretation that a scratch was not a bite. But the health department was the legal authority, and as Bud's custodians, we were required to obey. The woman finally agreed that Bud could be observed in "lock up" for ten days in lieu of county placement.

Administrative Assistant Jane Sherer agreed to quarantine Bud, but she lived in another county and this was not acceptable. He must be quartered in Jefferson County. Resident Monitor Shelia Sullivan agreed to take Bud home, as she already had a cat. The health department accepted this home incarceration. All of the above was duly reported to Dismas Charities Inc. corporate office. I was relieved to hear that our solution was acceptable, and we did not get a knee-jerk ban on all animals at all centers, as would have been the case at a state correctional facility.

Ten days later, Bud was released from home incarceration. He received his shots and returned to a cat's life at St. Patrick. Two weeks later, we received the news that he apparently was not neutered. Shelia Sullivan's female cat was "with kittens."

AJ was designated as Kevin's cat, and almost from the beginning, Bud was Alvin's cat. Alvin, tall, muscular and tattooed, with long, sandy hair, spoke in wry comments and hailed from a rural area of southern Kentucky. Every morning at five, Bud came to the backdoor howling. Alvin would feed him, and Bud would leave for a few hours pursuing community recreation. He would then return to visit and nap. In the afternoon, he would hunt and bring his kill to the men in the smoking tent. When the backyard closed for visiting, he would come through the front door and sleep in a lobby chair unless an ambitious staff member unceremoniously evicted him.

Bud quickly let AJ know he was top cat at St. Patrick. He selected the best napping place, took over both food dishes and let AJ know with a quick punch in the jaw that he was in charge. Sometime in the spring of 1999, AJ gave up the struggle and left.

Bud knew everyone's schedule. He became involved in a mural painting on Main Street, a block away. Alvin was chief artist, and where Alvin went, Bud went. Bud would walk over with the crew and supervise all afternoon. When Alvin painted the plaque listing the participants in the mural, he added Bud's name.

Bud did not like changes in his routine. When the backyard was resurfaced and everything moved, he stalked around showing his displeasure. He would perch on the smoking tent and glare down.

Alvin explained that Bud was showing power over the other residents, his littermates.

Bud shared the excitement when Alvin erected a basketball goal. During the first few nights residents used the goal, Bud sat on a garbage can and watched the basketball as it bounced around.

Bud got in a fight and his back leg was badly injured. He went to the vet. Alvin and some other residents faithfully administered his medicine. A few weeks later, his leg was re-injured. The vet called and said that if Bud weren't neutered, the fights would continue. Residents out-voted me on this issue many times, so I did not discuss it. I wanted no more vet bills. I had him neutered.

I went to the backyard and told the regular cat-watching crew the verdict on Bud's manhood. I also told them this could happen to residents of St. Patrick who fight. They assured me there would be no fights, understanding my warped humor and knowing fights were virtually nonexistent.

In July, Resident Monitor Sheila Sullivan told me that Alvin, pending parole in August, wanted to take Bud home with him. She said Alvin was going to live on a seventy-five-acre farm and that he was very concerned about what would happen to Bud when he left. I told her to have Alvin see me.

Instead, I received a "home and a job placement" form in my mailbox for Bud D. Cat. The job was as a professional bird killer for Birds R Us. The home placement was with Alvin Ramsey, stepfather. I concurred.

On the day Alvin left for parole, so did Bud. When I arrived for the day, Resident Monitor Al Russell (AJ's namesake) told me two residents had left on parole, Alvin and Bud. The residents missed Bud, but no one disagreed that it was the proper thing to do. They knew how important Bud was to Alvin. Even the sages in the smoke tent agreed during their daily commentary on center events. Still, the backyard felt lonely, as it does when any valued individual leaves.

Les Petit and Les Grand Miracles

Around the time I completed college, I developed a desire to learn French. This desire was deepened by graduate work exploring European social thought. I did not pursue French for several reasons, including the fact I had no natural aptitude for languages, a tin ear for subtleties of sound, an inability to imitate sounds, an Appalachian accent and an F in third semester Latin.

In late 2000, Dismas gave me the opportunity to attend the International Conference on Community Corrections (ICCA) in Ottawa, Canada. ICCA provided excellent information on correctional programs that work, and additionally, the participants were constantly exposed to the French language. I came away from the conference with a determination to implement some new programming for the residents and, despite my limitations, to learn French.

For the next year, I spent my commute time (two hours) listening to French language tapes, my lunch hour studying French language books and fell asleep with a French easy reader. On weekends, I rented subtitled movies. Progress was slow.

Both staff and residents questioned my sanity as they observed me in my car replying to French tapes. The constant exposure to French sometimes caused me to make sudden, out-of-context comments — in

French. For no reason, I might say, "L'autre cote de la rue" (the other side of the street) or "Vous avez vendu une chemise a mon pere" (You sold a shirt to my father).

I frequently attempted to practice my French on Resident Monitor Al Russell, who spoke five languages. Communication broke down with my accent and limited vocabulary. However, we did have the following exchange often:

Me: "Est-ce qu'il y a un fou dans la maison?" (Is there a crazy person in the house?)

Mr. Russell: "Oui, il y a beaucoup de fous ici." (Yes, there are many crazy people here.)

At this point Resident Monitor Darryl Woodson would begin speaking Spanish, and Assistant Director Yvette McCollum would walk off.

This is all a wordy introduction to my subject of large and small miracles. Working with a high-risk population brought many disappointments. With some regularity, however, small events took place that led us to believe that perhaps hope existed. These miracles kept us going.

One Saturday in May, a staff member found the VCR full of fabric softener. After Resident Monitor Roy McKinney completed an investigation, he notified me at home just after three that afternoon. It appeared that that a couple of residents had a dispute over whether to watch a movie or sports. The sports fan, in a fit of rage, dumped fabric softener into the machine. As all the information was second- or third-hand, I elected to place the two prime suspects on restriction until the VCR was replaced and we had a bill of sale and receipt. The suspects would be released when this was completed, with no follow-up punishment.

Voila! At five, a new VCR with receipt and bill of sale was delivered to the front door of St. Patrick. *Un petit miracle!*

In February, we received a young parolee, Jacob, from out of state. He had the poor judgment to reside in a remote Appalachian county and become involved with the daughter of a powerful county official. He compounded his error by committing a number of relatively minor criminal offenses and upsetting some other powerful and temperamental individuals. Six days after his arrival, he was scheduled to be in court in the distant county. He faced several obstacles: 1) He had no money. 2) He had no family support. 3) He knew no one in the state with a car who could or would take him such a distance. 4) There was no bus service to that county. 5) If he failed to go to court, his parole would be revoked.

Jacob called and requested his court date be delayed. The court clerk told him the court date would not be changed and it was his problem. Jacob and his counselor looked at all of the options and came up with a possible solution. He would go to work for one of the day-labor temporary services. He would renew his driver's license. He would rent a car. Normally, we did not allow residents to work for these types of organizations. Frequently, the work was not stable, and other employees sometimes had drug and alcohol-abuse problems. Normally, we did not let residents rent cars. Unusual problems, however, called for unusual solutions. We gave him the go-ahead. In four days, he had saved $138. It was time to call for a car rental. Because he did not have a credit card and had not maintained employment for the last year (he had been in prison), not one of the dozens of companies he called would rent him a car. He had one day to find a solution.

It was Monday night, and Jacob had to be in court Wednesday morning. I had a sudden inspiration and called a nun employed by Dismas, Sister Laverne. I did not get halfway through my plea when she stopped me.

"You want me to take him to court, and of course I will," she said.

"You will have to start at five in the morning, and it's a hard four-hour drive."

"Look, when someone has done all that they can do, it's time to help," she responded simply.

I looked at the telephone in disbelief. This was *un grand miracle*, which would soon be followed by another.

At that month's population meeting, I discussed the stress I suffered when residents told bold-faced lies. I discussed the relationship between claiming responsibility for your wrongs and personal courage.

"You know you are lying, I know you are lying, and you even know, I know you are lying."

The speech was more a personal tirade than an expectation of results.

On Sunday a week later, I received a call at three in the morning. Some residents kept going in and out of the bathroom and would not settle down. Staff suspected drugs or alcohol.

"Take them downstairs," I ordered. "Give them all alcohol breath tests and urine screens and write them up for being out of bed. Tell dayshift to 'drop' the house (perform urine tests on the entire population)."

On Monday, I knew what happened within ten minutes of arriving at the center. Information moved through the center very quickly. It had been a craps game in the second-floor bathroom. I even knew who owned the dice and the names of the men running the game. One of the culprits was at the Central Monitoring Office, leaning on the window ledge talking to dayshift staff. He asked me how my weekend went.

"It was fine until I was called at 3 a.m. about you and your friends."

"I don't know about them, but I was just using the bathroom."

I looked over my glasses and glared. "Right."

That afternoon, I was reviewing the culprit's file when he came to the door. I asked him in.

"Right here it is," I said, pounding on his arrest record. "Three past charges of loitering for the purpose of gambling."

"That's why I came to see you. I'm guilty. It was a craps game. I was in on it."

I just gulped. Before the next day passed, four more residents crept into my office and confessed. And when the stained-glass window was accidentally broken in the bathroom a few weeks later, two confessions and agreements to pay for the repairs occurred before the working day was half an hour old. These were *les grand miracles!*

On the Friday after the stained-glass confessions, I saw or heard from four former residents, and all were doing extremely well, working, saving money, drug-free and involved in positive ventures. One man, Tonda, described the success of his school-age children and his new involvement in a community theater. Another man told me he no longer even throws trash in the streets. What a wonderful way to end a week!

Every day, large and small miracles occurred at St. Patrick. These miracles, rays of hope and sources of joy, kept staff going through the bad times. They affirmed our work and reminded us that the people we served were of value.

The Beat and Bang Construction Company

Directors have different areas of interest, and the favored areas tend to get more attention than the others. The utilization of residents' work skills was one of my preferred tasks. I personally interviewed all pre-releases (inmates) to acquaint myself with their skills and limitations, which gave me information on the best community-service work placement for each individual. I also acquired other useful information in the process.

I started with questions about medical problems and allergies. I explored current charges, anticipated parole date, education level and incarceration history. A movement from less secure to more secure facilities was always a subject for inquiry.

I posed questions about their work assignments in past prisons, knowing from experience that Kentucky State Reformatory staff only placed the best workers at the KSR firehouse and that landscape assignments at one particular minimum-security facility frequently went to the less enthusiastic workers. I determined if janitors were of the "shade tree" variety or if they knew how to strip and buff. I then questioned residents about work history outside of prison. All of this gave me an idea about what I could expect.

Frequently, I received letters from inmates wanting to come to St. Patrick. I always answered my mail, giving them the accurate answer, "You need to go through the prison classification system. We do not select residents. They are sent to us via classification."

Several years ago, I received an unusual letter from an inmate at a state minimum-security facility, Bell County Forestry Camp. The man, Rocco, spent most of his letter discussing his interests and abilities as a painter. He also discussed his recovery from alcoholism in an unusually sincere way. Always looking for a good painter, I was interested. I asked Luke, who had served time with Rocco, about his character and received a very positive response. While having no control over incoming residents, the center needed the labor this man could provide, and I decided to mention it to placement personnel at the Department of Corrections. Rocco apparently was needed elsewhere, and they sent him to another community center.

Rocco wrote me from his new placement, and I wrote back, reminding him that the decision had been made and it appeared he would not be moved. He later appeared before the parole board and received a twenty-four-month deferment, making him ineligible for the community center program. He was returned to prison. Shortly before becoming eligible again for community placement, he wrote again. I e-mailed the state's placement coordinator and requested a painter and indicated Rocco was a painter and eligible for community placement.

A month or two later, someone from the Kentucky Department of Corrections called. She said they had inadvertently sent Rocco to Dismas Charities St. Ann that day, but I could trade for him if I wanted. Director Jennifer King, burned from some of my past trades, was not interested in a swap. They did not need a painter, however, and she agreed to send him to St. Patrick. When Rocco arrived, I made it a point to talk with him. After corresponding for more than a year, I was curious. Rocco, in his forties with medium build and short, thinning hair with a touch of gray, was personable and greatly enjoyed talking. Time would determine if the effort made to bring him to St. Patrick would be fruitful.

Rocco proved to be an outstanding painter, the best I had seen in the prison system. Skilled, neat and very fast, he also had an eye for color that would be the envy of any interior decorator. He had, not only skill, but a tremendous sense of humor. Rocco first conceived of the Beat and Bang Construction Company.

When I received a man who claimed construction skills, I moved carefully. First, the legitimacy of any project had to be evaluated. Kentucky inmates can perform maintenance work required for the upkeep of a building but cannot perform major construction work that would change the value of the property. After determining the legality of a project, I then needed to evaluate the skills of the untried worker. I normally gave him small jobs to assess his abilities, rarely assigning a complicated task unless I was desperate. Such was the case of Everett.

The inspecting fire marshal, in her infinite wisdom, decided that the refrigerator under the staircase was a fire hazard. It did not matter that her office had approved the location for the past six inspections or that few people had ever seen a refrigerator burn. The refrigerator was under a staircase, and that was against code. We had to relocate it, and the only logical move was to build a closet for the offending appliance. The closet would not change the value of St. Patrick, but it would assure we could pass the required fire marshal inspection.

I put Everett to work. He was moving along reasonably well from studding to the installation of drywall. About this time, St. Patrick received a returning resident, Welch, a skilled maintenance worker. Everett started on the drywall finish work.

Of the many skills I do not possess, taping and finishing drywall is one of them. I once taped several rooms in my father's house. My sister, who restores plaster for a living, avoided looking at the walls to keep from flinching. It was so bad that my father remodeled the rooms to cover up my work. Everett's work looked like mine. I pulled Welch aside, and we took a look.

"Can you do something about it? But don't hurt his feelings."

"He already asked me if I could straighten it out."

Within a few days, the closet looked wonderful. I did not even have to hurt Everett's feelings.

Everett and Welch moved from project to project. They repaired shelves in the basement and then moved on to the neglected rectory next to St. Patrick. Rocco named the pair the Beat and Bang Construction Company and sometimes assisted them.

After the original St. Patrick congregation moved to the suburbs, the old rectory had been leased to Dismas Charities, initially to house individuals suffering from HIV. Catholic Charities later subleased the rectory to house refugees. After several years, Catholic Charities determined they could better serve refugees in individual apartments. At the same time, there developed a waiting list for parolees in prison awaiting community center placement. Dismas Charities decided to meet this need. The old rectory had developed a number of maintenance problems requiring attention before the building could be reopened for parolees. About the time the repair work was completed, Everett served out his sentence, and painting began in earnest.

When painting became the primary task, the residents renamed the work crew the Splish and Splash Painting Company. We made every effort to keep the improvements inexpensive and were delighted when Maintenance Supervisor Dave Dalton gave us access to the many gallons of donated paint in his storeroom. The paint included overruns, strange colors and worthless cans used as tax write-offs by various companies. Rocco referred to the cans as "dead dogs," painters' slang for a collection of this nature. Rocco went through the "dead dogs" and created designer colors by mixing and blending. The result was a paint job comparable to ones found in expensive renovations of classic buildings. I was truly impressed.

The old rectory was ready for beds and furniture. The Splish and Splash Painting Company of Welch and Rocco moved on to annual outside projects, leaving the task of moving to others.

Two assigned residents started moving in lockers and beds from a vacated Dismas facility in the neighboring Portland community. The residents found the lockers bolted together in sets of four and quickly realized they would not fit through the stairways. They formed the Crash and Crunch Moving Company and began the challenge of taking the lockers apart and reassembling them. With some help from other men, the company's grand finale was to move a couple of 500-pound boiler parts out of the rectory basement.

The only item not perfect for the anticipated parolees was the carpet. The carpet in three of the rooms was so badly damaged that Dismas contracted with a professional carpet installer to have it replaced. The rest of the carpet was simply ugly beyond redemption. For six months, I searched the population for a carpet installer without success.

One day, I was prowling around Mr. Dalton's cavernous warehouse and spotted stacks of used carpet. I renewed my search for a carpet installer. A newly arriving halfway back came to us with an explosive temper but a lifetime of experience laying carpet. The halfway back formed the Goop and Glop Flooring Company, and in less than two weeks, they replaced the ugly rugs with used but attractive carpet. The building was ready.

Each of us finds our greatest reward in the accomplishment of something difficult. Doing meaningful work while incarcerated is not a punishment; it is a privilege. The residents in the various "companies," through skill and hard work, created something beautiful and contributed to the welfare of the residents who followed them. The rectory reopened to provide attractive, comfortable and clean living space for twenty parolees.

The rectory door

The rectory interior

How We Captured the Great Albino Manatee or What Is Recreation?

Leisure in the backyard

Nearly all inmates call the sentences of incarceration imposed by judges "doing time." This is for good reason. The sentence mandates the inmate spend a portion of his life in a place and under conditions not of his own choosing. In addition, correctional facilities are frequently boring places, and time moves slowly.

Correctional administrators are challenged to help the inmate make positive use of time and provide opportunities for him to pursue interests not in conflict with the security of the facility. Under the best of situations, inmates spend structured time in work, education and treatment. This still leaves many hours of leisure.

It is challenging but essential to provide positive uses of leisure for the incarcerated. For a high percentage of inmates, leisure time prior to incarceration was associated with substance abuse, gambling and unlawful activity. The violation of institutional rules is highest during the hours when most inmates are not in structured activities. Positive life changes for these individuals require a new use of leisure time.

In the years I worked for the Kentucky Department of Corrections, two wardens discussed with me the importance of inmates' leisure time. Warden Bill Dotson said, "Prisons are boring places. At least once a month, do something crazy." Warden Betty Kasulke, referring to serious incidents that happened at Kentucky Correctional Institution for Women on Halloween and New Year's Eve, said, "Provide positive recreation on holidays, or they will provide their own."

I took the advice of these experienced wardens seriously; however, designing a successful recreation program at St. Patrick proved to be difficult. The physical plant consisted of a small backyard, a small TV room and a building not designed to meet the needs of fifty active men with differing interests. As the leisure time was theirs, I accepted much input from the residents on the planning of activities.

Each month, a committee of interested residents and I would plan the next month's activities. Regular events included evening programs such as Alcoholics Anonymous meetings, organized sports and trips to the gym at another Dismas facility. Special events ranged from visits to the planetarium and art museum to fishing, swimming, bowling and skating. Some events were completely new to some of the men. Holiday events also were scheduled.

St. Patrick had three parties each year, Halloween, Christmas and Valentine's or St. Patrick's Day. Committees of interested residents volunteered to plan the events, which took almost a month each. Decorations, menus, music and events for children took a great deal of work and coordination. The planning was as much a part of recreation as the actual event, and the men learned much in the process.

Many men preferred work projects or gardening as spare-time activities. I noticed this was especially true of older men. Other residents preferred carpentry, art or special projects. Two men built a life-size casket for Halloween. A man painted a sign for a non-profit agency. Drawing was popular. One man painted a regulation shuffleboard court on the backyard pavement. Shuffleboard became a permanent activity. Sometimes I would go on the backyard and find the area busy with men involved in a variety of crafts or activities.

One summer, Rex requested a baby pool. I remembered Warden Dotson and his admonition to do something crazy. Not wanting this strange item to show on my petty cash ledger, I bought it for the center. Rex spent most of the summer lying in the wading pool. As he was slightly overweight, only his nose and stomach cleared the water. We referred to him as the "Great Albino Manatee."

Some activities were spontaneous. Somehow, we acquired two worn-out parts of a ping-pong table. The smoke tent soon became a ping-pong parlor with twelve men waiting, watching or playing. (We later bought a table.) The next evening, a street-cleaning crew found a somewhat deflated football. Soon, five men were throwing football.

The younger residents especially enjoyed organized sports. The pre-release residents with longer sentences were the backbone of the softball and basketball teams, which Resident Monitor Darryl Woodson dubbed the "Sky Hawks." Because St. Patrick had only thirty or forty pre-releases, compared to sixty and eighty-seven at the other two Dismas centers, the Sky Hawks lost more games than they won.

In 1996, the first season of play, the Sky Hawks lost all their games during the regular basketball season. The first game played in the tournament that year went into double overtime, and to everyone's surprise, even their own, the Sky Hawks won. The final game for the championship went into triple overtime, and the Sky Hawks defeated the valiant Diersen Knights for the trophy. Not since the Mets won the World Series had the sports world seen such an upset!

Resident Monitor Roy McKinney coached the Sky Hawks for several years, and no matter what their record, he was their most loyal fan. In good seasons, he made logbook entries about how they mangled the "Diersen Ducks" or the "St. Ann's Chickens." In the 2001 season, he pronounced the Sky Hawks "undefeated" — because they did not defeat anyone. Sky Hawk jokes became another recreational activity.

What is recreation? Recreation is many things — swimming, gardening, building a casket, playing basketball and, yes, a thirty-two-year-old man lying in a wading pool.

The Phantom Pooper and Other Mysteries

This story comes with a couple of disclaimers. First, it should be Rated R. Second, as it has been my practice to attempt to capture our residents in all of their diversity, I would be remiss not to discuss some of their antisocial acts. This story is not about murder and mayhem. It is about bathroom behavior, sexual peculiarities, vandalism and petty theft.

One morning, a very distressed resident came to see me. Kenny, a massive man of six foot two, wore size five-X shirts. Prior to incarceration, he sometimes worked as a stand-up comedian, specializing in African-American humor. He attended college in a study-release program and was majoring in drama. As he had little financial assistance, he worked as a St. Patrick bathroom janitor, which provided him $1.25 per day, rather than the $.75 per day received by inmates who only attended school.

Kenny took pride in his work, attacking soap scum energetically. On the morning of his visit, he discovered that someone had left a bowel movement on the shower floor and felt it was important to share this with me. He expressed his anger in no uncertain and very descriptive terms.

"Oh," I said without any shock at all. "We have a phantom pooper."

I explained the psychological dynamics. People who display this type of behavior frequently have been sexually abused. They are not able to express anger in adult ways, nor are they able to discuss or resolve individual differences. I went on to explain how individuals with this type of personality express anger in the way a non-verbal young child might communicate emotions. In effect, the person has never grown beyond the emotional age of a young child. I told Kenny that the program at St. Patrick was difficult and required more emotional maturity than this type of person usually has. Phantom poopers did not stay long at St. Patrick. In a few weeks, he would be gone.

Kenny wanted the problem discussed at the upcoming population meeting but was not sure it would do any good. We decided to put the topic on the agenda anyway. At the meeting, I carefully and without judgment explained the psychological dynamics of a phantom pooper. The population was both amused and more educated about human behavior. They did not fall asleep. The behavior stopped.

Dealing with this kind of problem was not so simple at state prisons. The men in the severely disturbed units at Kentucky State Reformatory and young first offenders at Blackburn, a state minimum-security facility, presented much more of a challenge. One inmate at KSR was famous for his bathroom behavior. His nickname by staff and inmates alike was Shitty Bill. Another KSR inmate brushed his teeth with feces. He breathed on an officer and asked him how he liked his new toothpaste. He shortly found himself in the segregation unit, a section of the prison that serves as the prison's jail.

Another of the many strange incidents at KSR was the case of a young man who severely injured himself by putting a toilet-bowl brush up his anus. When asked why he did this, he replied, "I'm getting the Klingons out." Captain Kirk was never so creative.

Bathroom misbehavior extended beyond fecal matter. One prison tradition was to use toothpaste to paste pornographic magazine pictures on shower walls to serve as masturbation aids. The inmate left the picture for the janitor to remove. This was extremely prevalent among the young first offenders at Blackburn.

When I transferred to the women's prison, I was lost. I did not know any of the staff or residents. When the KCIW staff took me on a tour, we went to the small unit that housed several male inmates assigned to maintenance work. The embarrassed tour guide apologized when we found a toothpaste picture in the shower. I laughed and said that this was something I understood. KCIW started to feel more familiar.

Still, I was enthusiastic about a Dismas rule that prohibited all pornography. There was seldom a toothpaste picture, and staff did not have to deal with opening lockers and finding pictures of female genitals staring at them. The mail rarely brought lewd photographs or the kinds of items received in the mail at KSR, everything from pubic hair to human secretions. St. Patrick could handle an occasional phantom pooper.

Other antisocial acts that directors face are vandalism and the destruction of property. Vandalism is an immature demonstration of rage. The lower the level of anger in the facility, the less vandalism one will find. Vandalism also is proportional to the level of investment residents have in the facility. We had an extremely low level of deliberate vandalism at St. Patrick. I can count only a few significant incidents in six years. In these cases, investigations usually revealed the culprits, and the residents paid for the destruction.

The accidental or careless destruction of property happened more frequently. Staff expected residents to report these incidents, and they usually cooperated. About twice a year, an over-enthusiastic weightlifter tipped the weight machine and put a hole in the wall. The resident reported the problem; other residents made repairs, and life went on. A stained-glass window in the bathroom was accidentally broken, the only one ever broken by a resident. Two residents quickly took responsibility and agreed to pay for the damage.

An incident on the backyard did not go so smoothly. The basketball went over the back gate. Four residents decided to push out the bottom of the gate and let a smaller friend through, rather than ask staff to assist. The gate opener snapped, resulting in damage costing $500. The culprits lied about the incident, probably fearing they would be required to pay for the damage. One pre-release paroled before the investigation was completed. Three pre-releases were transferred. One parolee who was involved finally confessed after a week of restriction. He agreed to pay $100 toward the repair of the gate.

Of all the antisocial acts directors must attempt to resolve, theft is the most prevalent. Searches usually are futile, because the thieves have good hiding places or manage to get the property out before it is missed. Mass restrictions are seldom successful and punish the innocent as well as the guilty. They also increase the overall hostility level of the population. Short, well-timed restrictions sometimes work if the property is missed immediately, which is seldom the case.

In October 1999, while attending a Halloween party dressed as a nun, I received a call from the center. Someone had vandalized a man's locker and stolen a gold chain and his money. As the staff duty officer was new and the staff inexperienced, I went to the center in full costume, habit flying behind me. I held a population meeting still in costume, cussed out the thief and left. The property never showed up. If there is a good method of resolving theft in a center, I never found it and neither did the swearing nun.

Residents come to correctional settings from every type of background. Their emotional problems and ethical systems are as unique as their faces. Not all the mysteries that arise will be solved. Staff will never find the phantom pooper. Other mysteries must be faced individually — with ethical instruction, education and, finally, a sense of humor.

– PART THREE –

Holidays and Special Events

Special events are an important part of programming at a correctional facility, never more so than at Christmas. For this reason, the majority of selections in this chapter involve Christmas events.

Christmas does not stop for the incarcerated or their families. Feelings are close to the surface for many reasons. Some offenders cannot remember a Christmas when their father was not drunk. Anxiety is at a peak. At St. Patrick, staff and residents both endured and celebrated the season.

Cops and Robbers

by Kathlene Bello
Dismas Charities St. Patrick
Assistant Director
1997-2000

St. Patrick's Team

The director and the assistant director of Dismas Charities St. Patrick shared a simple understanding. Director Gail Chandler was the "good cop." She orchestrated social activities, holiday events and community projects and led the center to numerous Clean Block championships. As assistant director, I was the "bad cop." I dealt with security, enforced house rules and administered disciplinary sanctions. Therefore, it was no surprise that Special Olympics Kentucky endeared itself to the residents of St. Patrick when they held an event that tossed their beloved assistant director into the icy waters of the Ohio River in the middle of February. The St. Patrick men were quick to raise and donate money in support of the event to get a chance to see their "bad cop" freeze herself half to death. They had a blast.

Later that year, when another chance to be involved with a Special Olympics event presented itself, the St. Patrick men were very interested. This time, however, it would be all up to them. In order to participate, they had to raise $50 each and form a team of up to twenty men. This event, the UPS Plane Pull sponsored by the Law

Enforcement Torch Run, was a competition to see which team could pull a full-size 747 jet twelve feet in the fastest time. It was a true test of strength and teamwork.

Stepping up to make the event a little more interesting, I challenged the men of Dismas Charities Diersen Center and Dismas Charities St. Ann to form their own teams and compete against the St. Patrick team. The fund raising began, as did the taunts and dares.

After several car washes, candy sales and a month of dropping their spare change into a bucket, the big day arrived. Together, the three centers raised $2,504 but had only thirty-six men to compete. It was time to make a big decision: Should they form one team of twenty men to have a good showing at the competition or keep two teams of eighteen men each for their own personal match-up. All of the other thirty-nine teams were twenty members strong, and most were veterans of the five-year annual event. They would not be easy to beat, even with a full team of twenty men. Last year's winners, the Jefferson County Police Department, made it well known that they intended to take home the trophy again. The Dismas teams, St. Patrick and Diersen (each supplemented with two men from St. Ann's center), agreed to team up evenly at eighteen men apiece and challenged each other to a pizza party prize.

It was a cool day at the airport, raining nonstop, but spirits were high. More than $65,000 had been raised, and hundreds of people turned out to show their support and their muscles. Although the event was open to anyone, most teams were comprised of local law enforcement. Area county and city departments were well represented each year, but this was first time they faced a team of known offenders. This year, egos were on the line, and the local law enforcement officers did not hide the fact that they felt imposed upon — it was, after all, their event. This feeling did not go unnoticed by our men. The tension was evident.

As the day went on, some of the Dismas men questioned if they should compete at all. They had raised the money, so they had done the important part of helping Special Olympics. Having a history with the law, they felt threatened by the thought that they might upset the local officers. Others felt that they should pick the twenty strongest men to form one good team to have a chance at a decent finish time. But, when their turn came, they stuck to their plan of eighteen men on each team in a friendly competition for pizza and stepped out on the runway proudly and maturely. They went there to have a good time, to represent their team well and show good sportsmanship in competing to benefit a greater cause.

St. Patrick's team stepped up to their line determined to do their best. Their first attempt was less than encouraging, and the Diersen team taunted them. As the plane lined up for the team's second attempt, the men dug in.

"Get low everybody, get low and lean in!" one man shouted. They quickly crouched lower.

"Everyone lean into the rope!" another screamed. "Lean in when you pull, so we're not pulling against each other!"

They were coming together. They were psyched. Somewhere between the time they chose to stick to their plan and the time they took their places on the line, these eighteen men had made a decision inside themselves. They were going for it. The timer called, "Go!" The team lunged forward. The plane rolled, one foot, three feet, six feet and crossed the line at twelve feet. The timer called the time. "5.88 seconds!"

Gasps came from the crowd. "No way!" "Impossible!" "Nobody's broken six seconds!"

Nevertheless, they had done it. They were in first place with a new event record. The Diersen men came running as the teams celebrated with hugs and jumps for joy.

With two fewer members than any other team, Dismas Charities St. Patrick won the event and set a new division record. They were presented with a trophy and got their team photo on a billboard in downtown Louisville. More importantly, they had proven to themselves and everyone else that they could succeed. They could put their efforts together for something bigger, something more important than their own individual benefit. They learned that in doing so they could be proud of themselves.

As all the other teams, even the somewhat emotionally wounded police officers, cheered and congratulated them, these men realized that they were not much different from those other teams. Their futures started with the great thing they had done on that runway, and it proved that they were good people capable of doing good things — of doing great things.

Will the Elf
Wear Tights?

The controversy started in a Christmas committee meeting. Ted had agreed to be the Santa Claus. As we reviewed the chaos of the previous Christmas party, we decided that Santa needed help. The combination of selecting an age-appropriate gift to give the right child and posing for photographs was more than one Santa could manage. The committee recommended an elf to assist. Manuel, a burly black man with a large voice and a remarkably un-elf-like appearance, was selected. The jokes began at once with a suggestion that he wear tights. Manuel adamantly stated that he would not wear tights and that a discrete Santa hat would be the absolute extent of his costume. Ted and Manuel were a good pair, and the event went smoothly.

Ted and Manuel were both still at St. Patrick the following year, and both were again on the Christmas committee. While Ted wanted to give a repeat performance, he was willing to let someone else have the job. "Salesman" secured the position. Manuel declined to be the elf again, so the search began for a replacement. Word went out to the population, and Joey was the unanimous selection. Joey, at four foot eight, weighed about a hundred pounds. I wondered if he would do it. Remembering the Halloween party, his counselor Mike Doyle said, anyone who would wear a pumpkin on his head would be an elf. I remembered that Joey and Ted had gone head-to-head over who would be the vampire. Ted won, but Joey would not be outdone. He wore a pumpkin on his head. Mike was right. Joey accepted.

Joey was nineteen years old and had been a gang member. Early in his stay at St. Patrick, he received a subpoena to testify against a fellow gang member. He was very frightened, as he perceived danger to himself and his family. One night on the backyard, we discussed his fears at length. He told me that one person charged was guilty, another innocent and his testimony could make a difference. I told him he did not have a choice about testifying, he was legally required to do so and that it was the morally correct thing to do. He agreed and said that he must be a man. I remembered seeing him walk back into St. Patrick with the weight of the world on his small frame.

The Christmas committee met again. Unexpectedly, Joey asked if he could wear an elf costume if his family bought him one. This brought a flurry of jokes about tights. I assured Joey that if he would wear it, an elf suit would be found. A few days later, "Salesman" donated $40 toward a Santa suit. I went to a costume store to buy one and also found an elf suit for $14. As an afterthought, I threw in a pair of green tights.

For the next week, the favorite topic of conversation was whether Joey would wear the tights. He asked me if he had to wear them. I assured him that it was totally up to him. There was so much discussion and so many jokes about the tights, I began to regret buying them. On the day of the Christmas party, the entire landscape crew where Joey worked returned that evening discussing the tights. Apparently, they had spent the day trying to convince Joey to wear them.

The Christmas party was very crowded. Santa and his elf were due to come down the staircase at seven-thirty. At eight, people were still being served, and Santa was struggling with his eyebrows. The crowd grew restless. The music went off. The loud speaker blared, "On Dancer, on Prancer, on Donner and Blitzen…." Santa and his elf came down the staircase. Santa's eyebrows were straight. The elf wore green jogging pants. They arrived at the Christmas tree. Once there, the elf dropped his pants, revealing a pair of bright green tights. The children were thrilled and loved their gifts. Everyone enjoyed the party. The photographs were great.

After the party, Joey was jubilant. He said he had never had so much fun. He reported that a small girl told him that she liked elves.

He felt ten feet tall.

Mr. Doyle and I reviewed the events. We discussed the tights.

"You know," he said, "it took a real man to do that."

I agreed.

Santa and the Elf

The Most Amazing Santa Claus

Santa dancing

It was just an ordinary December day. Parole Officer Anita Sanchez called with just an ordinary halfway-back referral. (The halfway-back program is an alternative to incarceration for parolees and probationers who have violated their release.) I picked up my pen to collect basic information. She started with his name, Rory Doe.

"Rory Doe!" I exclaimed, dropping my pen. "Surely you aren't sending me Rory Doe for Christmas!"

I followed this with a few very nice but well-chosen expletives.

"I know," she replied. "I wanted to send him back to prison, but my supervisor, Roy Hamilton, wouldn't let me".

With a notable lack of Christmas spirit, I cried, "Surely, Roy Hamilton wouldn't do this to me at Christmas!"

I called Roy Hamilton and got his answering machine. To the machine, I expressed my thoughts about spending Christmas with Rory Doe, but it provided little satisfaction.

I remembered Rory well. Square-featured and handsome, he had lived at St. Patrick several years before. He managed to complete the program by a most narrow margin. He was probably the most annoying parolee ever to pass through St. Patrick. He was, not only arrogant, but contemptuous of authority. I remembered Rory's abrasive personality and the relief of staff and residents alike on the day of his departure.

Rory arrived. This time he was grateful to be at St. Patrick rather than in prison. He knew he was on a very short leash, and his attitude was respectful. I was not convinced but had better things to do than be concerned about the miraculous transformation of Rory Doe.

I needed a Santa Claus and an elf for the Christmas party. A couple of days later I began looking for volunteers for the Santa role. To my great surprise, Rory volunteered. Our youngest resident, "The Kid," agreed to be the elf. The St. Patrick Christmas crew was in place. Meanwhile, Rory got a job as a waiter. He arranged to have the night off to play Santa.

Rory and "The Kid" did an excellent job. Child after child climbed onto Rory's lap. Some hugged him and a few cried. All received a present. A hundred photographs were taken. The party was successful.

At his place of employment, the manager named Rory "waiter of the month" for December. In January, his second son was born. Watching him hold his baby and seeing him play Santa gave me an entirely new perspective on this individual. He completed the program on a little more solid footing than previously. Two years later, he came by St. Patrick to discuss a donation of asphalt to the center. He now owned his own company and experienced no further difficulties with parole supervision.

The Spirit of Christmas

St. Patrick decorated at Christmas

It was always gratifying when residents looked beyond their own circumstances to reach out to others. I had such an experience one December. At our December population meeting, the residents always are reminded to look out and care for each other, as the season is difficult for everyone. That year, not only did they look out for each other, but for the refugees next door.

As usual, we spent much of December planning the annual Christmas party. In order to ensure that there would be a gift for each child at our party, I normally purchased a few extras in each age group. When the party was over, there were gifts leftover. One of our residents asked if we could take these gifts to the refugee children residing in the rectory next door to St. Patrick. I contacted Catholic Charities, received permission and obtained information on the children. They reported there were nine children in the facility, all under the age of ten. Mary, the onsite manager, said she also needed assistance in showing the children how to decorate a Christmas tree.

Four residents went — one dressed as Santa, one dressed as an elf and two wearing Santa hats. The experience touched us all. The children were tiny, grateful and remarkably well behaved. One small boy, about three, shared his candy cane with his little sister. An eight-year-old girl opened her package. It contained a coloring book and crayons. While not ungrateful, she looked disappointed.

I asked her mother if we could try again. She came over, and I gave her another package. Very seriously, she handed the crayons back. She received a tiny Teddy bear. She clutched the bear throughout the visit. The other children were very pleased with their toys, holding them, showing them to each other and rolling the cars on the floor in the universal manner of small children.

The St. Patrick men prepared the ornaments for the tree. Very carefully and each in turn, the children hung the ornaments on the tree. Even the smallest children joined in. They were so calm, so orderly and so careful, we almost held our breaths.

In addition to the children's gifts, our residents took up a collection for the adults. From their meager resources, they collected $62, which they gave to Catholic Charities earmarked as "something for Christmas" for these strangers in our land. Our men were able to experience the gift of giving, and two Somali families learned of our customs.

Oscar the Grouch Meets a Leprechaun

The Leprechaun

Oscar, in his late forties with tattoos and a gray, grizzled beard, epitomized the stereotype of a seasoned white "convict." Best described as salty, he enjoyed complaining far more than he enjoyed any organized recreational activity. In the outside world, he was a burglar and a drunk. Inside, he was a skilled maintenance man, mechanically minded but untrained. He could fix anything with duct tape and WD-40. He was a lousy citizen but an excellent inmate.

As was my practice, I interviewed Oscar upon arrival for a job placement. As he reviewed his prison job placements, I was impressed. He was frequently assigned to very responsible positions in boiler rooms and sewage-treatment plants. In my experience, only men who were skilled and dependable received such assignments. He did not attempt to excuse his long criminal history and candidly stated that he was a drunk. In spite of a six-page arrest record, his prison resume was outstanding. I assigned him to maintenance, and he soon involved himself in the life of the center.

When we started planning a St Patrick's Day party, Oscar decided to participate and enter the "Who is wearing the most green?" contest.

Not only was this out of character for Oscar, but for all men I had met like him. Salty, grouchy, middle-aged maintenance men just did not dress up. They stood back and made disparaging remarks about those who did.

Since this was our first experience with a St. Patrick's Day party, the planning committee looked for ideas. At Halloween, a masked "Jason" always greeted the children, handed out candy and helped with children's activities. The committee decided a leprechaun could assume the same role at the St. Patrick's Day party and searched for a candidate. Julius, a short muscular black man nicknamed "Catfish," volunteered. An appropriately dressed resident leprechaun would certainly be a hit, both for the children and residents.

Catfish and I took a trip to a costume store, where we found a splendid leprechaun hat, huge green bowtie and a "Kiss me I'm Irish" armband. Not finished, Catfish asked if the store had leprechaun shoes. I remembered that at Christmas I had seen elf shoes with curled-up toes. (I had been trying to buy these shoes for Santa's elf for four years, but no one would ever agree to wear them, so I never bought them.) A quick trip by the clerk to the store attic, and we had the shoes. I then remembered that our Christmas elf suit came with green tights and a green tunic and asked Catfish if he wanted to add these items as well. Of course he did!

The leprechaun was a huge hit, and he even wore green tights. The party progressed nicely. The question came up as to whether the leprechaun was eligible to enter the "Who is wearing the most green?" contest. I ruled that he was, as any adult male who had enough guts to dress up like a leprechaun, complete with tights and elf shoes, deserved it. The decision also was in line with the center tradition of allowing the men wearing center masks to participate in the Halloween costume contest.

The leprechaun won first prize. Denny, who dressed in a green housecoat as a St Patrick's Day flasher, won second, and Jack, with a green top hat and green skivvies sticking out, won third. Oscar did not even place.

Oscar left the party and retreated upstairs to pout. A stream of residents slid into my office and told me Oscar was extremely angry. After the party was over, I went home. I figured Oscar would cool down by the next day, and besides, my feet hurt.

The next day, Oscar filed a grievance and complained to all within earshot about violations to his constitutional rights. Most irate because I allowed Catfish in the contest, his ravings contained racial overtones. Jack came to me twice volunteering to calm Oscar down. Luke talked to me three times. I was pulling my hair out wondering why an adult man would act in such a way over something meant to be fun. I could only speculate that to enter such a contest was so out of character for him that he had to get angry about something. Anger was a safe and familiar emotion for him.

I knew I had to address the issue before the weekend. That afternoon, I asked Assistant Director Kathlene Bello to talk to Oscar. She had not made the decision to allow the leprechaun in the contest and did not have a stake in the outcome. She and Oscar talked for a long time and aired, not only the leprechaun issue, but some other complaints as well. I resolved the other complaints before I met with Oscar. I told him about those issues before we tackled the difficult leprechaun complaint. Our conversation went well, and we agreed to disagree.

A few days later, Oscar came to see me. He said his temper had gotten completely out of control and he needed to see a doctor. Recognizing the urgency, the appointment was made for the earliest possible date. After the doctor's appointment, Oscar's disposition radically improved. I realized how improved a few days later.

Jack told me someone had written racist graffiti about a white resident in a bathroom stall. Catfish, the bathroom janitor, found it and discussed it with Oscar because Catfish did not want to be blamed and he felt responsible for the bathroom. Although they are of different races, Catfish and Oscar were equally offended. Together, they went to Jack to ask him to paint over the words. I opened up the tool cabinet. The offending words disappeared. They had worked together.

While the leprechaun issue may seem very trivial, it is the material out of which prison riots and assaults materialize. This strange incident illustrates the difference between some large prisons and a community correctional facility where staff and residents choose to communicate rather than use brute force. People talk, agree to disagree, examine issues and grow to a point where they can solve problems together.

"Big John" Meets St. Nick

"Big John" arrived at St. Patrick one January. Several residents had known John at other places and eagerly greeted him. It was apparent that these men liked and respected him. Over the months, I grew to know John well. As an inmate, he would be with us for more than a year. John, with dark brown skin and long braided hair, was a mountain of a man, weighing 300 pounds and standing over six foot one. It did not take long to understand the reasons for his popularity with his peers or see the insecurity he covered with anger. I learned that his parents were both deceased and that a history of cocaine addiction was long and troublesome. He had a positive work ethic and was assigned to the city landscaping department.

While John worked well in landscaping, it was evident that the hard physical labor was difficult for him. In August, he requested to work in the center, and his request was granted. After his assignment to work as a center janitor, John began talking regularly with staff. He discussed issues, plans and concerns. He always kept up with the news. I called him the "town crier" because he and a circle of others discussed the news every day, but John always knew the facts. I saw his level of trust increase and his level of anger decrease.

In early December, I started looking for a St. Patrick Santa. I asked other people while John was in the room, but I never asked him. John had been overweight his entire life, and I had reason to believe the Santa Claus issue might be painful for him. I also speculated that the Santa suit might not fit him anyway, and that would be embarrassing.

Several days later, John came to see me in a mood to talk. He shared an experience from third grade. His teacher told him he was to play Santa Claus. He refused and his teacher called his mother. Not only was he required to play Santa, but he was punished, both by his mother and his teacher. I saw the embarrassed, overweight child in the big man's eyes. I could not comprehend what his teacher was thinking and how she could equate John's obvious humiliation with the spirit of Christmas. John told me that this was why he did not volunteer to be Santa Claus. I told him I understood, that it was his choice and someone else had already volunteered.

John may not have wanted to be Santa, but he was very interested in Christmas preparations. He did not know that at 3 a.m. on Christmas, a package with his name on it would be put under the tree like it was for every St. Patrick resident. He kept dropping hints. He told me that at the prisons, everyone got candy and a $5 canteen card. I gave him a noncommittal "uh huh." He kept hinting.

Meanwhile, I was very busy. In October, I ordered knit hats and socks. I located overstocks of soap and shampoo. A kind woman donated sixty sets of underwear and sixty large chocolate Santas. Another person called with a donation of cigarettes. We had a box of picture frames in the basement. I found a bargain on gray sweatshirts and ordered sixty: forty-four in size extra large, fifteen in size two-X and one in size four-X for "Big John." When I went to pick them up, there were only fifty-nine sweatshirts; John's had not come in. It was December 23, the company was closed, and I had no shirt for John. I sent Administrative Assistant Jane Sherer to a store specializing in clothing for large men.

Mrs. Sherer called from the store. "They have one purple four-X and one gray five-X, but it is $25!"

John was going to get a shirt like everyone else. "Buy the $25 shirt."

When John's counselor returned from Christmas break, John was waiting for her. He told her that he was going to save his new shirt to wear to the parole board, as it was the nicest thing he owned. I had never seen him so positive and so mellow; he even shampooed the carpet on his own initiative. I believe Christmas at St. Patrick played an important part in healing his spirit, and I appreciated the opportunity to do this special thing. It is important to acknowledge the child in all of us — the hurt child, the sad child and the child eagerly awaiting Christmas.

Christmas in Kenya

Vihiga Children's Home in Kenya

In September 1999, my daughter, Tara, applied for a cooperative-education placement at Vihiga Children's Home in Kenya, East Africa. Director Pricilla Agesa wrote back and said she would like to have Tara; however, she had no money to pay an employee. Although Tara needed a paying position, she was interested in Africa and decided to go anyway. The three months turned out to be the most rewarding of her life.

The Agesas were a retired couple living on a fixed income. They were native to Kenya but educated in the United States. As Quakers, they were committed to helping their fellow citizens. The poverty in this area of Africa is unlike anything we see in this country. They had taken in fourteen boys who were homeless or abused and housed them in the only facility they had, a dung hut where the children slept three to a bed. The boys were, however, in a much better situation than many of the children in the countryside or those children without homes. When Tara made home visits to the families of some of the boys in care, she never saw a bed or a child with a change of clothing.

Tara wrote to me about the situation. With her limited student means, she donated money to the facility several times. Ten dollars assured the boys meat for a month. Another donation replaced the dangerous outhouse. She sent me a photograph of a small boy who lived next door to the Agesas. His only clothing was a shirt in tatters. Starvation swelled his little stomach. At her going-away party, she went next door and picked him up so that he could share the rice and beans. She called him "Ya Ya You" because he always greeted her in broken English as he tried to say, "How are you?"

I shared the photograph with the men at St. Patrick in November. They expressed a desire to share their good fortune with someone else and agreed that the needs in Africa were a worthy cause. St. Anthony's Outreach, a neighboring agency, had received a donation of about fifty soccer uniforms, which had been stored there for several years. Also available would be children's toys leftover from the upcoming Christmas party and some children's T-shirts that had been donated to St. Patrick. We only needed the postage to get the items to Africa.

The men collected money, and we added to it the photograph money from the Christmas party. One man donated his entire month of state pay, which had been earned at $1.25 per day. Another man was concerned that the child in the photograph be helped. I assured him that I would let Mrs. Agesa know about this request. In all, we had about $130 for postage.

I wanted to send the four packages airmail, because I knew it would take the packages at least six weeks to get to Africa by surface mail and there was great danger that they would not arrive at all. Theft of mail is a common crime in Kenya. We had the first package weighed, and the airmail charge would be $94. We sent the packages by surface.

We did not hear anything for four months. In April, I received the front of a letter from Mrs. Agesa. It was marked "photographs," but everything in it was missing, even the back of the letter. In early May, Tara received a letter. In it was a photograph of the fourteen boys from the home, each wearing a pair of soccer shorts and a new T-shirt. In front of the boys was "Ya Ya You," wearing a pair of pants, something he did not own before.

This is a cause with no overhead, no salary and need beyond measure. Our men returned some of what they had received; they helped heal the human spirit.

– PART FOUR –

The Clean Block Contest

Part of the work of community corrections is to collaborate with local resources. A city agency, Brightside, was a favorite resource. Their mission was to promote civic pride by partnering with citizens to keep the community clean, green and environmentally aware. In 1996, with the corporate sponsorship of Bank One, Brightside implemented the Operation Brightside/Bank One Clean Block Contest.

St. Patrick entered the contest every year. Some years, there were as many as thirty-five contestants, and the event was very competitive. A team of judges met with each competing team on scheduled evenings in late July and selected the six finalists. A second group of judges selected the first-, second- and third-place winners on the first Saturday morning in August. A luncheon followed the final judging, and Brightside staff or a guest speaker announced the winners.

These stories tell something of the scope of work performed by the St. Patrick team, the residents who participated, their pride of accomplishment and the results of the annual contests. A resident wrote the final story in this section.

St. Patrick street garden

The Trash Man
1996

Directors are charged to run Dismas Charities facilities. Sometimes it felt as if St. Patrick ran me. This is how I lost control.

The St. Patrick neighborhood in August 1995 could best be described as Louisville's bowery district. At the railroad underpass one block from the center lay sheets of cardboard and old clothing. There was a constant stench of urine. Market Street was strewn with liquor bottles in brown bags and an occasional street person sleeping off his intoxication on the grass or sidewalk. Uncut weeds filled sidewalk cracks and grew around the edges of buildings. Every conceivable type of rubbish filled the gutters and walkways. When I arrived as the St. Patrick director, changing the neighborhood was not part of my plan, but I had not yet met Roger.

From an urban area, white and in his early fifties, Roger was only slightly my junior, and at six foot one, he also was one of the few men in the center taller than me. His age and size gave him the confidence to challenge me in a way that most of his peers did not. He had many skills, including the ability to grow almost any type of plant. (This skill was one of the reasons he was in our care.)

In November 1995, I assigned Roger to clean the area immediately around the center. Everything went smoothly for a while. Roger was very interested in the job, indicating that his home neighborhood did not have trash on the streets. He asked if he could clean the other side of the street and down Market a little way. I agreed. A few weeks later, he asked to clean the driveway into a neighboring company because cigarette butts from the backyard of St. Patrick often ended up in this area. Since it was our trash, I agreed. Roger came to me again, this time reporting the railroad underpass was filthy and that the stacks of garbage bothered him. He asked if he could clean it up. I said I would think about it.

In April, Diersen Center Director Robert Lanning sent me an application for the Clean Block Contest, a new program sponsored by the city's beautification program, Brightside. I saw the program as a way to legitimize cleaning the underpass and perhaps do some work on Main Street, which ran parallel to Market on the north. Besides, the winner would receive $1,000, and several projects needed funding.

A few weeks later, St. Patrick residents cleaned the trash from the Market Street underpass. On June 30, 1996, neighborhood vandals stole a car from Thirteenth Street, which runs to the east of the center. Since crime seemed reduced in orderly sections of our neighborhood, a cleanup seemed timely. Roger and other residents picked up numerous bags of garbage on Thirteenth Street, and he added a block of Thirteenth Street to his recently developed daily route.

Roger, now a familiar fixture in the neighborhood, started making friends and among them was the manager of Midwest Construction, our next-door neighbor on Market. He started sweeping the public sidewalk in front of Midwest.

As director, one of my monthly tasks was to obtain letters of support from the community when Dismas staff or residents were helpful. I asked Roger to secure a letter of support from Midwest, which he did.

Roger's cleaning route started to play dividends. He continued to clean up the driveway into a neighboring company. This company had filed suit to keep the zoning board from allowing Dismas to open the center at Market and Thirtieth. The bad blood between Dismas and this company was one of the things I was warned about when I was trained as director. I was very pleased and surprised when Roger reported this company also was writing a letter of support.

When the letter arrived, I contacted Dismas Executive Vice President Jan Kempf and Public Relations Director Bob Yates. They were amazed. Roger had accomplished something that attorneys and public relations specialists had not. I began to look at him differently. Perhaps he had something.

Roger next looked at the hedges across the street. "They look bad," he said. "I would like to trim them."

I said that they were on private property and not something I was interested in doing.

"General Leasing would really like to have them trimmed."

The next day I found another resident trimming the bushes, and Roger was sweeping the sidewalk nearby. I had to give them both a verbal thrashing.

"I didn't do it, but don't they look better?"

I had to agree.

The next day, Roger showed me stacks of pallets and trash in the alley behind an air-conditioning company on the opposite side of the street.

"This mess upsets the little old church people at the church on the corner. One of the other residents can have their family pick up the pallets."

I agreed but only if the company gave written permission. The company gave permission. The resident's family picked up most of the pallets. (A remaining few were used by a resident to build a home for the center cat…but that is another story.) A week or so later, Roger looked over at the air-conditioning company and commented on their ragged hedges.

"They look terrible, and the local street people sleep and do their business in the bushes."

I was noncommittal, but somehow the hedges were trimmed, and the company donated to us a couple of class-A street brooms.

Just prior to the Clean Block judging, we trimmed weeds and picked up trash on Main Street. We borrowed a utility cart from the company with the adjoining driveway (our former enemy) to carry our tools and transport the massive amounts of trash. A company on Main agreed to let us use their dumpster. The entire neighborhood seemed to be working as a unit. While we did not win the contest in 1996, we had something better.

Roger expanded his campaign. With only a little convincing, I agreed to allow the removal of a huge tree root from the St. Patrick side of the viaduct on Market Street. Six residents were diligently at work, and I walked down to watch. I found Roger sitting on a milk crate, enjoying other men doing the jobs he had created. Roger and I looked through the clean viaduct, on down past an alley to Fifteenth Street.

"You know, we really need to clean on down to Fifteenth. The trash blows into our area, and the locals throw their bottles in the bushes and…."

Luke mulching the tree with Roger on the milk crate

It Takes All Kinds
or
How We Created the Market Street Mural

St. Patrick residents painting the mural

Kerry, in his mid-forties, a few pounds overweight and looking a bit awkward in a ponytail, walked with the assurance of someone middle-class and well educated. He had adopted a criminal lifestyle at age thirty-eight, the result of cocaine abuse, depleted funds and creative fraud. Kerry's convictions multiplied, and as a result, the parole board developed a callous attitude toward his release. He received two back-to-back eighteen-month deferments and lived at St. Patrick for three years, close to a record. Kerry's creativity was not limited to the illegal, and during his time at St. Patrick, he was responsible for suggesting and implementing a phenomenal number of useful ideas.

Kerry never took advantage of his value to the center. He was involved in creative pursuits for their own sake, not for what he expected to gain. When Kerry came to me with an idea in November 1996, I listened. He wanted the St. Patrick residents to paint a mural on the

Market Street viaduct. While this sounded like a great idea, the procedures needed to secure permission for such a project seemed daunting. The project was placed on a back burner until after the holidays.

In January, after several phone calls, a helpful individual at Brightside, the city agency for beautification, provided specific information. A written proposal must be submitted, including blueprints for the artwork and letters supporting the project from every business on the block.

The Market Street viaduct, covered with graffiti, was an obvious eyesore, and the local businesses were delighted someone was willing to make a positive change. I suggested a cityscape of local businesses for the mural, and one of our residents, Ted, had the artistic skill to transform the idea into a blueprint. After viewing the blueprints, the businesses immediately wrote supporting letters. On February 7, 1997, the blueprints, proposal and reference letters were on their way to Brightside.

Two weeks later, I received a response. The city had no objection, but their attorney said the viaduct belonged to a railroad and the city could not give final approval. Several calls were made to locate the railway line that owned the viaduct, Louisville and Indiana Railways (L&I). A call to L&I brought a curt reply. L&I did not want the viaduct painted. We were back at square one.

The Brightside representative was contacted, and she called L&I, informing them that she represented the mayor's office on this issue. (This was true.) She sent L&I copies of the blueprint, and several weeks later, L&I relented. We were ready to look for paint.

We decided to start on the left side of the viaduct. Maintenance Supervisor Dave Dalton gave us numerous gallons of paint. Unfortunately, much of the paint was interior, and the exterior was in a variety of colors. As novices, none of us was aware that sixty gallons of the same color paint was required for a background, thirty for each side of the road. Rich mixed paint (and talked). Ted drew the outline on the wall. Kerry started painting.... And it rained. The project moved very, very slowly as we gradually realized the need for many more gallons of blue, our selected background color.

A month later, Mr. Dalton gave us more donated paint, again in a variety of colors. I took ten gallons of light-colored paint to a paint company. Under protest, they agreed to add blue dye to each of the cans, warning that the paints had different bases and would be different colors. We put the dyed paint in five-gallon buckets, mixed it together, and the new paint almost matched the first batch. Work could resume.

Dismas Public Relations Director Bob Yates saw the project as a great press opportunity and encouraged the scheduling of a painting party. We selected June 10. Six residents worked diligently under the observation of three different TV stations, and by the end of the day, the left side of the viaduct was beginning to take shape.

At about this point, it became obvious how varied were the skills and how many were the problems. Loafing and smoking took more time than actual work. It also became obvious that more white residents than black were involved in the project and that no one else could do detail work but Ted and he was becoming discouraged. In addition, of course, we were out of paint again. Ted, a large verbose man with multiple obscene tattoos, did not need a reason to procrastinate, but he had several. Problems needed to be resolved.

I contacted Brightside again and asked if the agency could secure some paint for us. My contact said this was possible. For three weeks, we waited for the paint. At about the same time the paint arrived, so did Presley. Presley was hard working, could do detail work for hours on end and had an artistic eye. He also happened to be black.

Ted and Presley became friends, working evening after evening after their regular jobs were finished. Presley completed detail work faster than Ted could do outlines, and the pressure of his friend tempered Ted's procrastination. One of our staff members, Resident Monitor Shelia Sullivan, contributed artistic ideas, outlines, detail work and more supervision to the project. The left side of the mural was completed, and the right side was well under way.

The next controversy was more easily resolved. Ted drew an angel to represent Heavenly Bodies car detail shop. He put a beard on the angel. I told him the angel looked like Jesus, and we could not use Jesus to advertise.

Ted walked away and Presley said, "I tried to tell him."

Ted returned and the beard disappeared. He painted the angel's face bronze, and it now could be either sex or any race. The manager of Heavenly Bodies was delighted.

Other local businesses began to come to the viaduct to look at their depictions and were uniformly pleased. Businesses donated paint the color of their buildings. The manager of Soapbox Laundry joined the parade to the viaduct and, not finding her business commemorated, expressed disappointment. A box of soap bubbles solved the problem, and the manager was pleased. The excitement of the businesses spread to others.

Community reaction to the mural could only be called wonderful. A woman came by with a photograph of her deceased sheep dog and asked that he be memorialized on the mural. She donated three gallons of paint in payment. Cars slowed, and drivers admired the project and shouted words of encouragement. The city bus stopped under the viaduct to let passengers look at the paintings. The bright blue mural was causing excitement, even in the neighboring community of Portland.

One day I walked into the Toll Bridge Inn in Portland. The restaurant owner and some regular customers were discussing the mural. Portland community leader Molly Leonard told me she wanted her viaduct painted.

The residents completed the mural in time for the Clean Block Contest with not a day to spare. Twenty-two residents worked on the project over six months. The mural was certainly a learning experience for the men and for me. We learned, not only the need for a great deal of paint, a variety of skills and a lot of perseverance, but the need for someone to help cut red tape. Even more importantly, we discovered how an idea and teamwork could transform a community.

We eventually painted four viaducts, including one for "Miss Molly" in the Portland community. The murals and their upkeep became annual projects and showpieces in the Operation Brightside/Bank One Clean Block Contest.

The mural completed

A Study in Black and White
1997

During the years I worked in correctional settings, the one problem that was ongoing and pervasive, affecting all levels of life for the inmate population, was the issue of interracial conflict. At best, it was a small annoyance similar to sibling rivalry. At worst, it was simmering and violent. It seemed any matter could be interpreted racially. An innocent administrative decision on food, discipline, canteens or recreation suddenly could be interpreted in racial terms and have very negative consequences.

Interracial conflicts moved and changed much like ocean waves, sometimes gently, sometimes like an incoming storm. The water was never still, especially in the 1970s when every prison in Kentucky worked toward integration. Some prisons moved to strict formulas, assigning black and white inmates to alternate beds. Honor dorms, where inmates had input into their assignments, became a challenge. One Kentucky prison had two waiting lists for honor housing in order to maintain a racial balance. The black waiting list was much shorter, causing a discrepancy of up to three months in the placement of black and white inmates who made the honor list on the same day.

While exact formulas provided systems that everyone understood, sometimes they seemed to defeat their own purpose. I tried to promote racial harmony by methods that were more general. I tried to be flexible and not lose my sense of humor. I encouraged staff to set the example and spend at least fifty-five percent of their time with residents of a race different than their own. I also tried to maintain a general balance in work crews and living areas.

In Kentucky prisons, black residents, who were in the minority, frequently staked out tables or areas as their territory. At St. Patrick, white residents, who were in the minority, did the same thing. This was particularly noticeable during population meetings, and it annoyed me. If an elephant is in the middle of the room it should receive acknowledgement, so I discussed the issue. I promised them if I did not have to look at this divided group at the next meeting, I would purchase a second microwave (which was needed). While expecting no long-term change, I was pacified when they complied and when I recalled the camaraderie existing between some residents of different races.

Kerry and Rich were friends. They argued and harassed each other like brothers. Kerry was white, Rich black. One day I told Rich to get his "brother" for some chore. It stuck, and Rich began to refer to Kerry as his brother.

Ted and Presley worked together every day while painting the Market Street mural. Presley was black, Ted white. Ted was sometimes unpredictably moody, and Presley was tolerant of him and provided friendship he needed.

When St. Patrick prepared for the judging of the 1997 Operation Brightside Clean Block Contest, the six residents most involved with the program were selected to assist with giving tours to the judges. The group consisted of Roger, Lonnie, Kerry, Rich, Ted and Presley. After plying the judges with coffee and doughnuts, we would show them the clean streets, new flowerbeds and the newly painted viaduct and later attend a luncheon where we would learn the contest winner.

It was a confident group, full of anticipation, sitting in front of St. Patrick drinking coffee that morning. The judges were very late, and the jokes were ongoing. There were remarks about the judges coming before the "winos" woke up. The sunflower growing in front of the center looked wilted, and we snipped it off at the stem and stuck in a fake flower. I made a remark to Presley about his "brother" Ted.

Rich asked, "What's with all the salt-and-pepper relatives?"

I just laughed.

The sun was shining. That morning they felt like family, like brothers. They had worked hard together, and we all anticipated showing off the work. I only wished that every day at St. Patrick had the same feeling.

The judges did not notice the fake flower, and to make the good feeling even better, we won the contest.

Presentation of the "Clean Block" award

Reggie, an Artist in Residence 1998

Reggie Painting

Success is difficult to duplicate, but the residents of St. Patrick and their director still remembered the sweet feeling of victory. Winning the 1997 Operation Brightside/Bank One Clean Block Contest affirmed the hard physical labor performed on Market Street. The bright blue mural reminded us daily of last year's victory. Could a mural on the nearby viaduct at Main Street give us the same result? We had one problem: Ted, our artist, had received parole and no longer lived at St. Patrick.

Ted designed the blueprints and outlined the Market Street viaduct mural. He painted the difficult figures of people and taught his peers techniques such as using a sponge to give the appearance of leaves in trees and twisting an artist's brush dipped in yellow to create flowers. Ted left the monotonous details like actually sponging in the leaves and drawing hundreds of lines to depict building bricks to others with more patience.

Ted was decidedly independent, far from modest and sometimes had problems with his peers. Roger, the resident landscaper, sometimes called him "Theodore Bundy" and not always behind his back. Ted ignored most insults and seemed to dwell primarily in his own world, oblivious not only to others but to time deadlines. The Market Street mural was awesome, but it took six months and a hundred threats (from me) to complete. I remembered procrastination as a trait to be avoided in the next designated artist.

I first met Reggie at Kentucky State Reformatory, where he worked in the inmate barbershop, which was under my jurisdiction. When Reggie came to St. Patrick, I assigned him to a landscaping position with the city and to a part-time job as the resident barber. I had no idea of his artistic skills. His landscape work did not go very well, and he seemed unhappy. Because I knew him from KSR and because he seemed to be having such a difficult time, I was especially concerned.

One day I was passing through the TV room and saw him sketching. His drawings were beautiful, and his talent was very evident. It was spring and time to start the mural on Main Street. Aha, I thought, I have been looking for you!

I told Reggie about the Market Street mural and that I needed an artist for Main Street. I asked him to go for a walk with me to see what we had done last year and to discuss this year's project. As we walked, I noticed that he was limping. When I asked, he said he had a congenital hip condition. I suddenly knew why he was having problems with landscaping. I offered him a less physically strenuous work assignment, a center janitorial position that would also allow him time needed to paint.

Reggie had his own ideas about what should go on the mural. As a black man who had grown up in the inner-city, he said inner-city children seldom get to see nature so this should be the subject matter of the mural. I told him Ted had done outlines and others had done the details. Reggie felt that if he was the artist, he should do the work.

It did evolve that he wanted company, someone to hold the blueprint, wash his brushes and support him in the long and tedious job. Williamson fit the bill. Like Ted's primary assistant, Presley, Williamson sometimes tired of Reggie's "artistic temperament." With both projects, I thought an assault might be committed before the project was over, but it never happened. Both sets of workers managed to work out their differences without mayhem.

Reggie planned his work carefully. He planned exactly how much he would do each day and each week. Reggie designed and single-handedly painted every artistic detail on the Main Street viaduct mural. Large panels depicted a seascape and water life with mallard ducks, and smaller panels displayed a sea turtle and a country fencerow. Reggie's project on Main Street, a viaduct twice the size of the one on Market, took three weeks...and it was beautiful.

In addition to the viaduct, Reggie painted a team symbol on the floor of St. Anthony's Outreach gym and decorated the fence behind St. Patrick with more mallard ducks. The project that will last the longest, however, was the refinishing of the cross that was reinstalled above St. Patrick in March 1999. The cross had been taken down in 1993 because it leaned radically and appeared ready to fall. Other construction was required on the front steeple to repair weather damage, and it seemed the ideal time to repair and reinstall the cross. I had discussions with several residents and indicated that we needed to repaint the cross because it would probably be there for another hundred years.

A few days later, Reggie came to see me. He told me that the paint must be removed down to the metal, instantly primed with a special paint primer and then painted again. I looked at him puzzled.

"I know what I am taking about," he said, slightly annoyed. "Don't you remember that I was in the Navy and spent my time sanding, priming and refinishing ships?"

I had forgotten but realized his advice would be sound. I talked with Maintenance Supervisor Dave Dalton and spent $80 on top-grade primer, paint and sanding belts. The cross soon was in shipshape and ready to be installed.

As the time approached for Reggie's meeting with the parole board, he knew we would need another artist. He recruited and recommended Alvin. In the same conversation, Reggie discussed the pride he felt in the Main Street viaduct. He told me the work in the neighborhood would spread, through the residents, to every part of Louisville, to every part of the state. I shared his dream.

St. Patrick took third place in the Clean Block Contest in 1998. Reggie left in April of the next year. The weather damaged parts of the mural Reggie painted, and more damage occurred when the railroad company removed one of the bridges in 2000. Alvin and "The Kid" repaired the damage, and in 2001, Rocco and Welch completely renovated the mural. One huge panel and the mallard ducks remain the same as when Reggie painted them. While the character of the wildlife scenes maintains Reggie's vision, the style of the new sections is different. When I look at the mural, I can almost hear him quarrel.

Seventy-Three
Stumps 1999

J.R.

Before   After

In 1978, I met JR when he arrived at the minimum-security prison where I was employed at the time. After orientation, staff assigned the tall, quiet black man to a dormitory that received little supervision because he exhibited maturity and good work habits. The placement was appropriate. JR paroled, and I did not see him again until he arrived at St. Patrick in 1999.

JR had changed little in twenty years. He had looked mature for twenty-eight and now looked youthful for forty-eight; the only change seemed to be a touch of gray in his hair and perhaps an additional ten pounds. While disappointed JR was again incarcerated, I was glad to see him. We discussed his parole revocation for misdemeanor driving while intoxicated, and I told him a bit about St. Patrick, including the Clean Block Contest.

Terry Ashbrook, the personnel director at Atlas Machine & Supply at 1400 West Jefferson Street, provided our inspiration for the 1999 Clean Block contest. I met Mr. Ashbrook at a meeting of the East Russell Neighborhood Association, an organization he founded in hopes of improving the community. While Main and Market had been littered with trash and debris before our cleanup efforts, the 1300 and 1400 blocks of West Jefferson near Atlas were even worse. Probably, they were the worst in East Russell and all of Louisville. (Main and Jefferson parallel Market to the north and south.)

These two blocks of Jefferson were the walking route between a large public housing complex and a popular liquor store. Mr. Ashbrook and his staff dealt, not only with unruly pedestrians and their trash, but most of the area's homeless people, some moving from the conditions they now found overly clean on Market and Main. I invited Mr. Ashbrook to St. Patrick to see the results of our labor. As we walked down Market, trash-free and bright with paint and flowers, an idea took shape.

When the 1999 Clean Block Contest rolled around, we were eager to improve last year's third-place position and saw an opportunity to improve working conditions on Jefferson Street as well. In our Clean Block application, we agreed to clean the two blocks of Jefferson and paint a viaduct by Atlas, in addition to our current commitments on Market and Main. Totaling seven city blocks, the project was very ambitious, even before we added another element — a 450-foot-long train to be painted on a retaining wall on Main. The extent of the challenge registered that day in March when we took our first trip to Jefferson Street and filled our half-ton cart with liquor bottles — three times in thirty-five minutes.

On a Friday in early July, touring our entire Clean Block area with JR, Roger and Alvin, I thought we had bitten off more than we could chew. Weeds were growing out of the sidewalks, the train was barely started, and the Jefferson viaduct was not complete. Worst of all, however, was a 100-foot-long flowerbed filled with liquor bottles, offensive trash and tree stumps. JR already had worked several long days on the stumps and had made barely a dent. The stumps were massive, intertwined and grew to the bottom of the bed.

All weekend long, I thought about the project. The preliminary judging would be the last week of July, and we had less than four weeks. I tossed and turned all night Sunday, thinking about the 450-foot train and the tree stumps. On Monday morning, I walked into the center and saw JR working out on the weight machine.

Before I said a word, he greeted me by saying, "I've been thinking about what we have to do and all of those stumps."

I felt like hugging him, and relief flowed over me. I realized I was not in this dilemma alone.

That day, JR and two other residents resumed labor on the flowerbed. Sam and Joe shoveled trash, filled carts with garbage and took it to a dumpster provided by Atlas. JR worked on the stumps with a handpick while we looked for a simpler method. A woman from the landscape division of the city tried to pull the stumps out with a truck, but they did not budge. A chainsaw, hatchet and hand-saw did not work either. JR broke the handpick; I bought a larger one. Tall, muscular and covered with sweat, JR stood in the flowerbed swinging the pick; he looked like Paul Bunyon. Late in the day, I counted the stumps, and there were still seventy-three.

For a while, JR and Sam worked mornings on the stumps, while Roger, Joe and Kevin worked afternoons. Each morning, I stopped by the flowerbed on the way to St. Patrick and then went to a local hard-ware store for more equipment and soft drinks, returning to give moral support. I even bought a splitting maul, which did not work either. We found no shortcuts.

The weather turned very hot. In ninety-eight-degree sun, JR kept digging. He swore at the paint crew across the street, sitting coolly on scaffolding painting pretty pictures, but kept going. Inch by inch, root by root, one by one, the stumps came out.

JR removed stumps while others helped in different ways. Alvin directed the completion of the painting. Max and Adam painted sixty-eight train wheels. Roger removed every weed from the sidewalks in a seven-block area. Kevin kept up with the trash, and Sam helped everyone.

On the last Monday in July, two days before the initial judging, the last root came out. Atlas gave us $1,000 for supplies, and one of our staff members, Resident Monitor Shirley McCubbins, filled the van with mulch, bushes and flowers. At 10 p.m. Tuesday, Sam and Daemon mulched as I supervised. The drunks of Jefferson Street walked by shouting words of encouragement.

By Wednesday night at 7:30, when the judges arrived to determine the finalists, everything was perfect. When we passed the beautiful flowerbed, I thought about the seventy-three stumps and the struggle and commitment of the man who removed them. The work paid off, and we made the run-off. The results of the finals are revealed in the next story.

Among the Truly Gifted
1999

Alvin painting

As director, one of the tasks I took on personally was to inventory the skills of each new pre-release and assign him to what I hoped was the most suitable job. I clearly recall many of these interviews. I was amazed at the skills of some individuals. Likewise, I was sometimes saddened to see a man grown to adulthood who had never been employed and did not have a skill or even a detectable interest in anything other than the moment.

I missed Alvin completely. I remember neither his interview nor his stated skills. I had a position open in the center serving meals, and I was relieved that someone was willing to take the job. I assigned him to serving three meals a day. Another resident brought Alvin's skills to my attention.

Reggie had been the center's artist for the Main Street viaduct, our project in 1998. He was meeting the parole board in April and knew we were planning to paint a mural on Jefferson Street for the 1999 Clean Block Contest. In January or February, he came to see me and said that he had found the next artist. Indeed, he had. I assigned Alvin as the third artist-in-residence at St. Patrick.

The first St. Patrick artist, Ted, had a wonderfully quirky sense of humor, reflected in his artwork as a dog howling at the moon, a man painting a tree and a seven-foot sheep dog. Ted taught me much, and among other things, I learned how to sponge-paint and how to make a flower. I passed on these techniques to others. Along with his skills, Ted had a major flaw: procrastination, a trait I wanted to avoid in future artists.

Reggie never procrastinated and planned his work weeks in advance. He had a completely different style than Ted. Reggie liked nature rather than street scenes and wanted inner-city children to see paintings of seagulls and mallard ducks. Reggie was very possessive of his work. When his able assistant wanted to help, Reggie told him, "If you want something to do, clean my damn brushes." Reggie's work was indeed beautiful, but his unwillingness to let others help made the project more personal than community. Because of the new project's size, the next artist would need to work with others.

The scope of the work for summer 1999 was enormous. Jefferson Street was dirty, and the constant flow of alcoholics through the mural site under the viaduct was disruptive. The art on the south side of the viaduct would represent the businesses on the street; the north side celebrated the public housing development Beecher Terrace and included a basketball court and players. Alvin would assume responsibility for all the artwork except the basketball game, which Resident Monitor Shelia Sullivan, a professional artist, would design and complete.

Alvin tackled the Jefferson Street viaduct with eagerness and creativity. He planned his work with a blueprint and stayed on schedule. He genuinely liked people, and his humor seldom failed. He outlined projects while observing his co-workers' skills. He diplomatically turned suitable projects over to others while completing complex sections himself.

Sponge-painting trees, by far the easiest job, required zero talent. One of Alvin's most faithful assistants, Marley, young and excellent with computers, became the sponge-painting specialist. After weeks of permitting only sponge-painting, Alvin finally allowed Marley to draw squiggly lines on tree trunks. Adam, a short, bald, middle-aged black man and former truck driver, had a steady hand. He painted details on the gas pumps featured on the support beams of the viaduct. The project was beginning to take shape.

I received a call from Dismas Charities Portland Director Linda Phelps. Shipping Port, a Portland-area business association, wanted the residents of her center to paint a train on the retaining wall at Fourteenth and Main. The wall was approximately two football fields long. She said her short-term residents had not the time, talent or interest to do such a project.

I was up to my ears in the Jefferson Street project. Plus, the removal of a bridge had badly damaged the Main Street mural, and the Market Street mural required a lot of repair from weather damage. I could not even imagine what Alvin would say if I added a 450-foot-long train to the summer's work. I told her I would talk to him, as I was sure he had the talent to do the project. I postponed this conversation for two weeks.

Alvin agreed to the train with no apparent reservation. He started making plans almost at once and completed the mural by the third week of July. It was seventeen cars long and about forty percent to scale. It had sixty-eight wheels, hundreds of crossties, an engine and caboose from the 1800s, and an engineer with a handlebar mustache. It captured the imagination of the entire community. Alvin and associates also restored the Main and Market murals and completed the new mural on Jefferson Street.

Alvin completed these projects with unfailing good humor and humility. I cannot say how fortunate I feel to have had this man at St. Patrick. For someone who started his art career as a graffiti artist, he traveled far. His natural gifts bloomed and developed. He became a real asset to the community in which he lived. He is among the truly gifted, not only among the fellowship of the incarcerated, but in the community at large.

St. Patrick took first place in the Operation Brightside/Bank One Clean Block Contest for 1999. A man who feared the arrival of Dismas Charities in the neighborhood, Rich Gimmel, chief executive officer of Atlas Machine & Supply, and Terry Ashbrook, personnel director, took twelve residents and three staff members to lunch to celebrate.

The train

I Was Only
Drunk Once
or
A Few Good Men
2000 and 2001

Roger was leaving for the second time in four years. Paroled just after we won the 1997 Clean Block Contest and returning just in time to help bring us to victory in 1999, he seemed to be a good luck charm for the center. The details of his parole revocation in 1999 had several versions, and I suspected there was some truth in each of them. Roger was now a senior citizen, and I hoped this was his last trip to St. Patrick.

Roger had a special place at St. Patrick. While I received several awards for the work of changing our neighborhood from a bowery to a pleasant, landscaped neighborhood, I never forgot Roger was the true initiator of the change. Although Roger sold an occasional carton of cigarettes to his peers at the center, he maintained strong beliefs about the ethics of his work. He believed that any transgressions with drugs, alcohol or accountability could cost us the program, and he was correct.

The only rules he bent involved his enthusiasm for a neat and tidy neighborhood. Bushes on private property would be mysteriously trimmed or shabby storefronts would be painted in my absence. His passion for a clean neighborhood supplemented creative landscaping ideas, some carpentry skills, a green thumb and the ability to convince other residents to do the work created by his active imagination. Roger invented the community-service assignment of "Clean Block worker" at St. Patrick. Since he had a personal investment in seeing the work continue, he started looking for his replacement early. Besides, a young, hardworking assistant would be Roger's way of putting his dreams to work while reducing his own sweat equity.

Roger recruited Lonnie by asking, "Hey kid, when do you meet the board?"

Lonnie told Roger his first parole date was in seven months. Roger mentally calculated a deferment of at least another year and became convinced his replacement had arrived. Throughout the spring, summer and fall of 1997, Roger thought up projects and sat on a milk crate watching his protégé mow, trim weeds, move dirt and sweat. Market Street looked great. Roger was happy. Lonnie was tired.

After Roger paroled in December, Lonnie was on his own. A remarkably quiet young man, Lonnie stood in contrast to his more vocal peers. He never complained, never asked for special privileges but counted it a privilege to work in freedom. His only method of questioning a strange assignment was a wry smile. Lonnie also had a green thumb. He held the position for about eighteen months, performing well until he paroled. He trained Kevin prior to his departure. Now it was Lonnie's turn to sit on a milk crate.

Kevin, slim, wiry and blond with the face of a choirboy, had an unseen disability. At the age of eighteen he had suffered a severe diving board accident that hospitalized him for two weeks, and he spent four and a half months in a recovery facility. The injury left him with a seizure disorder, a lifetime requirement for medication and a slight difficulty in translating spatial directions. The injury left intact reasoning from the written word, an infectious sense of humor, ability to get along with others, high energy and an excellent work ethic.

Kevin's strong point was trash. He quickly developed his own method for cleaning up a "trashed" street in the shortest possible time using his boot and a lobby pan, a dustpan with a long handle. He wore out a lobby pan a month until he started plastering the bottom of the pan with an epoxy. Kevin could not walk down the street without chasing trash. One moment he was in a conversation, the next moment he was running down the street chasing an elusive paper cup or plastic bag.

While Kevin was the best trash man to pass through the center, he did chop down all the sunflowers, and I missed having a person with a green thumb, regardless of how this skill was acquired. Roger returned in time to ensure a crop of sunflowers for 1999 but would leave in the fall, requiring a replacement.

While pondering Roger's replacement, I reviewed the types of workers residing in the center. Some had never learned to work or would not expend any effort to work even under supervision. Others worked well when directly supervised but seldom went beyond what they were instructed to do. I did not want either of these types. Neither did I want the third type of worker: those who knew how and what to do, applied themselves and went above and beyond — but always did it with a motive either to impress someone or to get some reward. Their goal was to accumulate letters from supervisors to impress the parole board or to acquire special privileges. These inmates reminded their supervisors in subtle or not-so-subtle ways that the supervisor "owed" them because they did their job well. (When I was young and inexperienced, I bit. When I became more seasoned, I reminded them that having a meaningful job in prison is a privilege.)

I was looking for someone who enjoyed the work for its own sake, put himself into his job a hundred percent, celebrated accomplishments and rewarded himself when all went well. I needed someone who worked well even if he had received a write-up and even if he knew you could do nothing for him. I wanted a partner in accomplishing the work, not someone reminding me that he was only getting $1.25 per day. Unfortunately, this type of inmate rarely comprised more than about five percent of any population. Roger, Lonnie and Kevin matched this description, and I needed one more.

Luke was a short, stocky man from a rural background and came recommended by Roger. He had the agricultural experience that was so helpful in Roger and Lonnie. (In my experience, reformed marijuana farmers were generally excellent workers.) After considerable thought, sometime in September 1999 I selected Luke for the job just in time for Roger to spend a month or so on a milk crate training him.

I was very satisfied. The sunflowers he planted on Market Street thrived. He grew squash and cucumbers. He painted and picked up trash. Market Street looked beautiful. I found Luke was more than just a hard worker. He put his heart and soul into the job and worked from early in the morning until late in the evening every day. Except for one day when he was flat on his back with the flu, he worked. He worked just as hard on the day he was turned down for his furlough as he worked the day his furlough was approved. He did not stretch accountability rules in any way. Although he frequently worked a block from a liquor store, he never strayed, which was verified through regular testing. He also demonstrated integrity.

Luke found an expensive gold watch hidden in a cigarette urn, obviously stolen and secured for later retrieval. He turned the watch in to staff, and they returned it to the rightful owner. He completely wore out his sneakers on his job and was pleased to take a donated pair rather than inconvenience his family. He tried very hard to respect the hardship his incarceration had caused them, unlike others who demanded packages and home-cooked food at every visit. He seemed to have evaluated his past mistakes and made a commitment to change. Luke also made me laugh almost every day.

Luke treated center property as if it were his own, and other residents understood, fearing to step on "Luke's" flowers or use too much of "his" weed-trimmer string. One day, a couple came by in a car, stopped by the sunflower patch on Market near Fifteenth Street and proceeded to harvest some of the flower heads. I saw him running down the street yelling and carrying a hoe. I followed rapidly. The couple must have realized he was serious, because the car sped off when he was still a half a block away.

He enjoyed griping about the number of consecutive days he had bologna for lunch or about extra-duty residents who did not double-bag the trash. He never griped about the new tasks I created for him almost every day. He never griped about the center, and he never griped about his job. He was one of the few residents who consistently appreciated the opportunities available at St. Patrick.

Luke and I talked almost every day as we made plans for the upcoming Clean Block Contest. He began to share his challenges with me. He was very concerned about the care his daughter was receiving. He discussed his commitment to sobriety.

"I only got drunk once. I was fourteen. When I finally sobered up, I was thirty-four and in prison."

This statement quickly became part of the rich history of the St. Patrick Clean Block workers, along with the milk crate and the sunflowers.

In 2000, St. Patrick did not make the finals of the Clean Block Contest. Dismas Charities Diersen and Dismas Charities St. Ann tied for first place, so at least we kept it in the family. I tried hard to keep up the spirit of the contest and told the residents we all had won because we had cleaner neighborhoods. The residents were not deceived by my attempt at good sportsmanship. Luke and Jack made a plaque for me. The plaque said, "In our eyes, we will always be Number One."

Luke

A Resident's Viewpoint
by Rocco Dilbeck
2001

Rocco Dilbeck

My name is Rocco, and I'm a resident of St. Patrick halfway house. I wanted to give my thoughts and observations on the annual Clean Block Contest, which St. Pat's enters each year. Other halfway houses and different neighborhood groups enter their areas and showcase the changes and improvements in hopes of winning the grand prize of $1,000…or so I thought.

My story actually begins in January when I first arrived here. I'm a painter by trade and was essentially brought here to do that. As I got settled in and got familiar with things, I saw a friend that I had met at another institution. His name is Luke. Luke had been here quite a while and filled me in on things, and that included the Clean Block Contest, which was to be held later on in the summertime.

For the next month or two, I did what I came here to do and that was paint. One of my projects was the rectory next door. At the rectory is where I saw the beginnings of the Clean Block Contest. I would take my breaks in the front of the building so I could look onto Market Street. I could look down and see Luke with his cart full of lumber, shovels, rakes and other tools heading down the street. At the end of each day, I would talk about what I was doing, and he'd do the same. This went on, and each day I would tease him about "you're doing too much." (That's slang, basically, for "Why are you doing all that work?") His only comment as he started down the street was that I'd get my turn pretty soon, and it was sooner than I thought.

When I was close to finishing the house I'd started, Luke and Mrs. Chandler, our director, began talking to me about painting and repainting the viaducts down the street. Off and on for a week or so, we toured the viaducts, and as we walked, Luke would show Mrs. Chandler and me the flowerbeds and boxes he had made. I quietly listened to him and Mrs. Chandler talk about last year's projects compared to this year and could see the ideas take form. It still didn't hit me that I would be a part of this thing until under one viaduct, I saw next to a mural, the names of former residents. They had painted and wanted to make the neighborhood a better place and also hoped to win the Clean Block Contest. This was approximately April, and for the next three months our project was slowly put together.

First of all, I should tell you that I've painted houses, churches, bridges, etc., but I'm not an artist. I wasn't sure about the murals and how they would look, but me and another resident named Welch got us a paint cart and began pushing it along with a scaffold and twenty-foot ladder down the street every morning. Now it was Luke's turn to laugh.

As the days turned into weeks, things started coming together. The first viaduct was completed and looked pretty good. Luke's flowers were coming up, but I found out later that we still had a long way to go. At different times of the day, I would listen to Luke and Mrs. Chandler talk about previous contests, and I also met a previous resident named Roger. In the beginning, I thought Roger was just a fast-food connection until I realized he had a special place at St. Patrick and especially with the Clean Block Contest. Now I had to listen to him and Luke talk about the dos and don'ts, and although I was doing my part, I somehow still didn't feel part of this thing, but Welch and me kept at it.

If nothing else, I would eat hamburgers, paint and get to be outside. Then came the Main Street viaduct, which was pretty shabby. Paint was peeling everywhere on the pictures, and there were large blank spaces with no pictures, and I just wasn't sure I could do it. You'll have to remember that at the first viaduct, we basically traced what was already there. This is where I really came to know Mrs. Chandler. She would stop by each morning and again on her way to lunch. We would talk, and I would say, "I don't think I can," and she would say, "I think you can" or "Try it and let's see." It was June by this time, and me and Welch were roasting out there, but Luke would come by and we would take a break and drink Gatorade, or Roger would come by and we'd eat hamburgers. I probably should tell you that Roger wasn't our only source of food. We had what I called a "Hamburger Jeanie" that would drop off food on occasion.

There was even one elderly couple that dropped off food on their way from church, and many people stopped to say "thank you" for doing work or to compliment us on how good it looked. I think along with all that and this one particular weekend, I finally felt good about the whole thing, maybe confident is a better word. There was this one particular big mural of a lake and mountains that was in very bad shape. I intentionally waited until the weekend to paint it because I knew there would be a lot of trial and error, and I didn't want anyone to see me. That weekend, I mixed and matched and would try something and get Welch's help on it and Luke's if he was there, and finally, on Sunday afternoon I had finished it. I was finally proud of some-

The Main Street mural

thing. Then later that Sunday afternoon, Mrs. Chandler called me to her office, and I got nervous. I knew the Hamburger Jeanie had been by, but I couldn't imagine what else I did wrong. When I walked in her office, she leaned back in her chair with a smile and told me it looked wonderful.

From that moment on, I really got into the contest. Also, things were beginning to move a little faster as we started running out of time. Luke had made parole and was waiting to start his program, and he gave me a crash course in the final stages of the Clean Block Contest. Mrs. Chandler was taking pictures, talking about scrapbooks and the route the judges would take, and I thought, "They really get into this." It was about two weeks and counting when we decided to enter Jefferson Street into the contest, making it a total of seven city blocks. It was up in the air because of all the construction going on, so the push was on to get things ready there too. Residents started really getting into it, and soon there were crews and details with brooms, weed trimmers and trash bags everywhere sweeping curbs and sidewalks.

We would string out 300 feet of hose in several locations to help with that part of the cleanup. With about two days to go, we picked our final route for the judges to take. Until that point, I still didn't really understand why it was such an important thing. Roger, Luke and Mrs. Chandler explained that we had to show off our good features and sidestep some not so good.

By then we had found out who else was in the contest, and I realized there was a bit of rivalry, which really made it a contest and an even bigger challenge. The evening was finally here for the prejudging. I sort of pride myself on not getting too excited about these things but found myself nervous as we headed out on the route with the judges. This is where it really became a group effort. The residents were talking and explaining about the neighborhood, the work and the pride that went into it. When it was over, we left with a lot of anticipation about whether we had made the finals or not. To top that off, we had to maintain the streets and other projects in perfect condition until we knew.

There were many discussions about "what if we win," "what if we lose," etc. But we kept up hope and three days later found out we made the finals. What's more, we would find out the winner at a luncheon downtown.

Saturday morning came, and once again, everything was in place. The new judges were younger and more into it, and for a while, I found it hard to talk to them and became frustrated, as everyone else seemed to be doing just fine. I finally made a connection to one of the judges and felt good about my input into that part of the contest.

So now we're at the luncheon along with the other finalists, and you could feel the excitement in the room. At first, I thought it was tension, but there were too many smiles for that. As I looked around the room, I saw the look of pride on everyone's face. Even though every team wanted to win, just being there was an accomplishment. Each team knew that, win or lose, things were better in their neighborhoods by them being there, and the little bit of competition seemed just that…competition. I'm sure there were a few that didn't see it my way, but there are always the few who know nothing about sportsmanship.

As they begin announcing the runner-up, there was a twist in who everyone at our table thought would win. With all the tough contestants still in the running for first place, the room was silent for a moment, and then St. Pat's won. At this point, I looked around the room and still saw the smiles on the faces, and that's when I really knew it wasn't about the $1,000 at all. The other teams filed out, maybe thinking about next year. St. Pat's filed out as the winner, and I suppose with pride comes a little gloating but it was all in fun.

It's October, and now the paint's all put up, but we have the colors wrote down. The flowers are beginning to die, but we saved some seeds. I'm sure a whole new set of residents are ready to do it next year. Myself, I'll probably be gone, but I think like my friend Roger, I may come around every now and then. Who knows, I may run up on some painter at one of those viaducts mixing and matching a color that he has no idea whether it'll work or not, and he might could use some words of encouragement and possibly a hamburger.

– PART FIVE –

Finale

"As strong as the human drive for food or air, is the desire for some type of immortality. Ultimately it is like writing your name in ice, on a hot July day."

– Author unknown

Sunflowers on Market Street

St. Patrick street garden

New Year's Eve found me in my office at 10:30 p.m. auditing resident files. The counselor responsible had made many errors, and consequently, the task proved frustrating. When I arrived home, my husband was already in bed, and I watched the Times Square ball drop on TV, completely exhausted and alone.

I thought, "I cannot do this anymore."

The next week, a young staff member and I stood in front of the center. A middle-aged man stopped his car and parked next to the building. With a lifetime history of alcoholism, a bad temper and lengthy stays in prison, he had been released from St. Patrick for almost a year. He looked sober and healthy.

"I just wanted to stop and thank you. I am doing great and you made the difference, all the times you kicked my butt."

He hugged me and left.

"How could you ever leave this?" said the staff member.

"How could I? This is what I do."

But, I knew it was time. The age of my parents, the desire to travel and the need to leave before losing the alertness to attend to people with many needs proved the deciding factors. I began the many tasks required for retirement and passing St. Patrick on to the next director, Steve Smith. On February 1, 2002, I retired. I laid my keys on the desk, threw my timesheet in the director's box and walked out the door. I said goodbye to the staff and residents of St. Patrick and to the sunflowers on Market Street.

Six months later, I sat with a woman at a picnic table at the east end of Market Street, fifteen blocks from the steeple of St. Patrick. A bouquet of fall flowers lay on the table between us.

A stranger walking by and noticing our animated conversation and thoughtful moments might think we were college friends or old neighbors. We were both tall, nearly six feet. She, with skin the color of ebony, wore a simple shift and sandals. She was reed-slim with very short hair so gray that the contrast with her skin resembled a work of art. About the same age, I wore jeans, large earrings, sneakers and a T-shirt bearing the inscription "Clean up Louisville." Someone had once said we were the opposite sides of the same coin.

Nevertheless, the relationship wasn't a traditional friendship. Sammie Ann, a frequent resident of the Kentucky Correctional Institution for Women, had cancer and resided in the drug-treatment section of a homeless shelter. I was her visitor. Other than this short relapse related to pain medication for her illness, Sammie Ann had been drug-free for eleven years and had not returned to the criminal lifestyle. It appeared we both were retired from the criminal justice system — just two old ladies talking about the past.

We exchanged gossip. I discovered the answer to a puzzle unresolved for many years, just how five women at KCIW acquired hepatitis C from one dirty needle. The death toll was now two with two others seriously ill. On the brighter side, I learned that Sammie Ann's four siblings, all former residents of state correctional facilities, had transformed their lives, leaving drugs and crime behind. The blessings of my life and the difficulties of hers were left unstated. As we talked, I pondered the common traits in our personalities and our very different destinies.

The visit over, Sammie Ann picked up her flowers and walked back to her little room in the homeless shelter to await next week's chemotherapy. I went to Paris.

Epilogue

St. Patrick cat

On January 28, 2003, Dismas Charities St. Patrick closed. A decision by the federal government to prohibit the courts from placing low-risk offenders directly into community housing had a significant financial impact on the agency. Dismas Charities elected to place residents and staff from both Diersen and St. Patrick in the empty Portland facility, significantly reducing overhead expenses.

Five days later, I drove by St. Patrick, vacant except for Tom, the center cat who sat on the doorstep waiting for residents who would never return. I drove to Dismas Charities Portland to check Tom's welfare. Staff told me that a counselor had moved Tom to the new facility, but he kept running away, going home to St. Patrick. I understood how Tom felt.

I drove by St. Patrick again on my way home, but Tom had disappeared. A paper cup blew across the road and joined other garbage that was beginning to collect on the sidewalk. I wondered if the neighborhood would be able to maintain the changes that the residents had worked so hard to implement or if Roger's dream would soon be buried under a pile of trash.

With or without St. Patrick, the lives of residents continue to change, progress, regress and evolve.

While I hear from some former residents regularly, others have disappeared or are preoccupied with their new lives. A state computer line, Kentucky Offender On-line Locator (KOOL), makes information on inmates now in the system readily available. I recently researched the forty-one men residing at St. Patrick on January 2, 1996. Only six — less than fifteen percent — were incarcerated.

Through the KOOL system and phone calls, I also researched thirty-six of the men and a cat featured in this book. Some of those who returned to prison were not anticipated, and some who have managed to stay out are equally improbable.

Adam – The truck driver *(Seventy-Three Stumps, Among the Truly Gifted)* Adam maintains an interest in church and is driving a truck again. He brought his big truck through Market Street several times to update us on his progress. He has not returned to prison.

Alvin – *(Bud Makes Parole, Reggie, Seventy-Three Stumps)* Alvin, on parole for three years, was rearrested and has been returned to confinement in a Kentucky correctional facility.

Beetlejuice – *(Beetlejuice and "The Kid")* The eccentric Beetlejuice absconded from St. Patrick, was rearrested and currently resides in a state prison.

Big John – *(Big John Meets St. Nick)* Santa's friend John paroled to a nearby state. On several occasions, he obtained a travel permit back to Kentucky. He stopped by to visit and is doing well.

Flowers on the "Clean Block"

St. Patrick fishing trip

Bud the Cat — (*Bud Makes Parole*) Bud happily traveled to the farm in southern Kentucky, purring all the way. He spent two years in active retirement, hunting shrews to his heart's content. One day he went into the woods and never returned. Alvin speculated that he had a hunting accident and that a rattlesnake or a large varmint ended his life.

Casper – (*Unmixed Blessing*) The escapee Casper is in a Kentucky State prison.

Denny – (*Unmixed Blessing, Oscar the Grouch*) The singing preacher Denny, released on parole, started his own company, became deeply involved in prison ministry and reunited with his wife. He is drug- and alcohol-free. On each of the several occasions he stopped by the center to see me, he said, "I am blessed."

Edwin – (*Ghosts*) The child abuse victim Edwin has not returned to the state prison system.

Halfway back, carpet installer (*The Beat and Bang Construction Company*) — The carpet man started drinking the day he got out but then regrouped and checked into residential drug treatment. He stopped at St. Patrick, showed me his three-month chip and said, "The program works, it made me ready." He has avoided prison.

Harry – *(Harry's Hemorrhoids)* The parolee Harry's parole was revoked, and he resides in a state minimum-security prison.

Jack – *(Ghosts, Unmixed Blessing, Can I Take My Daddy Home, I Was Only Drunk Once, Oscar the Grouch Meets a Leprechaun)* The model resident Jack married his girlfriend, Ann. He is working, paying child support and is involved in his children's lives. He serves as a volunteer firefighter.

Joey – *(Will the Elf Wear Tights?)* The elf Joey paroled to St. Patrick where he absconded his parole just as parole officers came to return him to custody for alcohol use. He hid in a locker and when found by a counselor, ran down the stairs and out the front door, injuring a parole officer. He is now in a state medium-security prison.

JR – *(Seventy-Three Stumps)* The stump man JR worked hard and saved his money for several years. He then received another DUI and is now residing at a Dismas facility.

Julius – *(Oscar the Grouch Meets a Leprechaun)* The leprechaun Julius is in a jail-release program in northern Kentucky.

Kenny – *(The Phantom Pooper)* The bathroom janitor Kenny served out the rest of his sentence and has not returned to prison.

Kerry – *(The Rope, Courage and Honesty, How We Created the Market Street Mural)* The creative Kerry elected to parole to St. Patrick where he obtained employment at a fast-food restaurant and completed the program quickly, moving to an apartment. Three years later, he has been promoted to manager and has been released from parole supervision. He keeps in touch and, other than having some medical problems, is doing extremely well.

Kevin, Clean Block worker # 3 – *(Tweedledum and Tweedledee, Bud Makes Parole, Seventy-Three Stumps, I Was Only Drunk Once)* Kevin violated his parole and returned to the prison system. He has now been released.

"The Kid" – *(Beetlejuice and "The Kid", The Most Amazing Santa Claus, Reggie)* The mascot "The Kid" is still in school, recently married and driving a beat-up car. He has not returned to prison.

Lee – *(The Rope)* The rope student Lee has not returned to prison.

Lonnie, Clean Block worker #2 — *(The Rope, A Study in Black and White, I Was Only Drunk Once)* Lonnie's wife sent a beautiful

Christmas card with a note saying all was well about a year after Lonnie's release. He has not returned to prison.

Luke – *(Ghosts, An Unmixed Blessing, What Is a Community? The Beat and Bang Construction Company, I Was Only Drunk Once, The Clean Block Contest)* The Farmer Luke paroled to St. Patrick and obtained a position with a nearby company, acquiring the position because the owner observed his work on Market Street. He trained Rocco to be his replacement, successfully completed the program, rented an apartment in Louisville and obtained custody of his six-year-old daughter. They regularly attend counseling as he struggles with the issues of single-parenting. He takes her to soccer practice, school events and worries about the scars of his alcoholism. He bought a truck, does landscaping jobs on the side and is saving for a house. His life is proceeding well.

Manuel – *(Will the Elf Wear Tights?)* The first elf Manuel has not returned to prison.

Marley – *(Among the Truly Gifted)* The tree-painter Marley has not returned to the criminal justice system.

Oscar – *(Oscar the Grouch Meets a Leprechaun)* The grouch Oscar is not in the Kentucky prison system.

Phillip – *(Tweedledum and Tweedledee)* The bad-tempered painter Phillip is not in the Kentucky prison system.

Presley – *(The Rope, How We Created the Market Street Mural, A Study in Black and White, Reggie)* Ted's conscience Presley returned to prison, paroled after a stay at St. Ann and from all reports is now doing well. On one occasion when he stopped by the center, he was driving a wrecker, and on another, he asked how long he needed to be out to work as a resident monitor at Dismas. He has made this his goal.

Reggie – *(What Is a Community? Men's Tears, Among the Truly Gifted, Courage and Honesty, Tweedledum and Tweedledee, The Fox and the Hound, Reggie, an Artist in Residence)* After release, Reggie struggled again with drug abuse and lost. His parole was revoked, and he returned to prison and currently resides at a Dismas facility. I saw him recently and he gave me an update. His mother died in 2000, his wife has stood by him, he has a new child and he still hopes to beat the specter of drug abuse.

Rex – *(The Next Generation, The Great Albino Manatee)* As reported in *The Next Generation*, Rex still resides in a Kentucky prison.

Rich – *(The Rope, A Study in Black and White, How We Created the Market Street Mural)* Kerry's friend Rich returned to prison and contacted the center when his mother died. His son was at St. Patrick, and Rich wanted to assure that he was able to attend the funeral. Rich has again been released.

Rocco – *(The Beat and Bang Construction Company, Reggie, The Clean Block Contest, a Resident's Viewpoint)* The painter Rocco began having problems with alcohol just after his release. His parole officer directed him to a treatment program, which he successfully completed. He resides in a three-quarter house where he receives support from his peers and is very active in AA. He works as a skilled painter.

Roger – *(The Rope, What Is a Community?, The Trash Man, A Study in Black and White, Reggie, Seventy-Three Stumps, I Was Only Drunk Once, The Clean Block Contest)* The trash man Roger has not had further contact with the criminal justice system. His wife is very ill and her care is his most important concern. He occasionally contacts me and discusses the years on Market Street. Approved as a volunteer at St. Patrick, he still keeps an eye on the neighborhood sanitation.

Rory Doe – *(The Most Amazing Santa Claus)* The Christmas curse Rory is the owner of a construction company and the father of another son.

Rocco's painting
of the rectory kitchen

The Rectory staircase with
color and painting by Rocco

Our neighborhood prepared for the
Clean Block contest

Sam – *(Seventy-three Stumps)* The helper Sam is not in the Kentucky prison system.

Ted – *(The Rope, Will the Elf Wear Tights?, How We Created the Market Street Mural, A Study in Black and White, Reggie, Among the Truly Gifted)* The procrastinating artist Ted had open-heart surgery a short time after leaving St. Patrick. The last time he came by the center, he brought his fiancée, a lovely young woman. He has not returned to prison.

Tonda – *(Les Petit and Les Grand Miracles)* The community volunteer Tonda continues to rear his three children, live in the inner-city and volunteer at the community theater. He has had no further contact with the criminal justice system.

Welch – *(The Beat and Bang Construction Company, The Clean Block Contest, Reggie)* The maintenance man Welch has not returned to the criminal justice system.

Wilson – *(Tweedledum and Tweedledee)* The con man Wilson is not in the Kentucky prison system.

Before: Market Street fence

After: Sunflower
seed and resident work

Flowers in Roger's garden

Dismas Charities Corporate Office
Louisville, Kentucky

The author of *Sunflowers on Market Sreet* wrote this book while working as a facility director for Dismas Charities. Dismas Charities has as its motto "healing the human spirit." Persons incarcerated in a community corrections center operated by Dismas learn that it is only by taking responsibility for one's actions that a person can change and turn away from victimizing others. Dismas Charities has as its goal to end the cycle of victimization brought about by a life of crime. When residents are released from a Dismas facility, they understand they will not have to return to prison if they respect themselves and others. Dismas residents learn this because they are given responsibilities and offered opportunities and then are held accountable for their actions.

Dismas Charities operates community correction facilities nationally. Headquartered in Louisville, Kentucky, Dismas was founded by Fr. William Diersen in 1964 to help men transition out of prison and back into the community. Fr. Diersen's purpose was to offer a hand up to those who are down.

In addition to community corrections centers, Dismas Charities also operates day care services for at-risk children. For more information please contact Dismas Charities, 2500 Seventh Street Road, Louisville, Kentucky 40208.

E. Gail Chandler

For the last seven years of her remarkable career in corrections, E. Gail Chandler was director of Dismas St. Patrick, a community correctional center where offenders prepared for return to society. With the wisdom and patience earned through two decades of working in state prisons, Chandler developed an exceptional Dismas program that helped many of these men start new lives. With Chandler's unwavering encouragement and belief in their worth, these men also transformed their inner-city neighborhood in Louisville, Kentucky.

Chandler began her corrections career in 1976, when she became Kentucky's first female deputy warden of a male prison — an eighty-bed facility in Frankfort. Two years later she moved to a larger, minimum-security prison and then to the Kentucky Correctional Institution for Women (KCIW).

At KCIW, she immediately was named in a class-action discrimination lawsuit on conditions in women's prisons, *Canterino v. Wilson.* This lawsuit became one of the two most significant federal cases on the rights of women prisoners in American history. During the thirteen-year course of litigation, KCIW became a national model facility for female offenders, and Chandler became a corrections expert in management, program development, classification, security, construction and litigation.

In 1993, Chandler went on to become the first female deputy warden at Kentucky State Reformatory, a 1,400-bed, medium-security male prison and one of the two oldest prisons in Kentucky. After state retirement, she became director of Dismas St. Patrick, rounding out her thirty-year career of daily contact with offenders at every custody level.

Chandler found the philosophy of Dismas Charities Inc. — "to heal the human spirit" — to be in keeping with her own experienced view of corrections. Through stories that are at once humorous, heartwarming and wrenching, Chandler provides a rare look inside the everyday life of some of society's least-known members.